ARTHUR RANSOME

Arthur Ransome was born in Leeds in 1884 and educated in Windermere and Rugby. His family spent their summers at Nibthwaite, to the south of Coniston Water. It was these early visits that gave Ransome his lifelong love for the Lake District, angling, natural history and the outdoors.

In 1902, Ransome abandoned a chemistry degree to become a publisher's office boy in London. He used this precarious existence to practise writing, producing several minor works before *Bohemia in London* (1907), a study of London's artistic scene and his first significant book. Others followed, including *Oscar Wilde* (1912) which led to Ransome being unsuccessfully but traumatically sued for libel by Lord Alfred Douglas.

During this period Ransome returned each year to Coniston, where he was befriended and mentored by W.G. Collingwood, John Ruskin's secretary. It was whilst staying with the Collingwoods that Ransome first learnt to sail.

An interest in folklore, together with a desire to escape unwelcome post-trial publicity and an unhappy first marriage, led Ransome to St Petersburg. There he researched *Old Peter's Russian Tales* (1916), before becoming a war reporter for the *Daily News*. He was thus ideally placed to observe and report on the Russian Revolution. He knew many of the leading Bolsheviks, including Lenin, Radek, Trotsky and the latter's secretary, Evgenia Shelepina. These contacts led to persistent but unproven accusations that he 'spied' for both the Bolsheviks and Britain. Unhappy about the Allied intervention in Russia, Ransome escaped with Evgenia to the Baltic States, carrying messages that helped to secure Estonian independence. Ransome married Evgenia and returned to England in 1924. Settling in the Lake District, he spent the late 1920s as a foreign correspondent and highly respected angling columnist for the *Manchester Guardian*. In 1928 he got to know W.G. Collingwood's grandchildren, whilst they were staying at Coniston. It was a combination of this friendship and Ransome's own childhood memories that inspired *Swallows and Amazons*.

Arthur Ransome went on to write eleven more *Swallows and Amazons* novels between 1930 and 1947. The sixth, *Pigeon Post*, was awarded the first Carnegie Medal for Children's Literature in 1937. All remain in print and have been widely translated.

He died in June 1967 and is buried at Rusland in the Lake District.

HELEN EDMUNDSON

Helen Edmundson's first play, *Flying*, was presented at the National Theatre Studio in 1990. In 1992, she adapted Tolstoy's *Anna Karenina* for Shared Experience, for whom she also adapted *The Mill on the Floss* in 1994. Both won awards – the TMA and the Time Out Awards respectively – and both productions were twice revived and extensively toured. Shared Experience also staged the original adaptation of *War and Peace* at the National Theatre in 1996, and toured her adaptations of Mary Webb's *Gone to Earth* in 2004, Euripides' *Orestes* in 2006, and the new two-part version of *War and Peace* in 2008. Her original play *The Clearing* was first staged at the Bush Theatre in 1993, winning John Whiting and Time Out Awards, and *Mother Teresa is Dead* was premiered at the Royal Court Theatre in 2002. Her adaptation of Jamila Gavin's *Coram Boy* premiered at the National Theatre to critical acclaim in 2005, receiving a Time Out Award. It was subsequently revived in 2006, and produced on Broadway in 2007. She adapted Calderón's *Life is a Dream* for the Donmar Warehouse in 2009, and her play *The Heresy of Love* was produced by the Royal Shakespeare Company in 2012.

NEIL HANNON

Neil Hannon is a singer, lyricist and composer. Although he is best known for recording and performing as The Divine Comedy, he has also written extensively for TV and film, including the music to *Father Ted* and *The IT Crowd*. He has collaborated with everyone from Michael Nyman to Tom Jones, and his recent cricket-themed side project The Duckworth Lewis Method was nominated for an Ivor Novello Award. *Swallows and Amazons* is his first venture into the world of musical theatre.

SWALLOWS
AND AMAZONS

adapted by
HELEN EDMUNDSON

with songs by
NEIL HANNON

based on the novel by
ARTHUR RANSOME

NICK HERN BOOKS
London
www.nickhernbooks.co.uk

A Nick Hern Book

This stage adaptation of *Swallows and Amazons* first published in Great Britain as a paperback original in 2011 by Nick Hern Books Limited, 14 Larden Road, London W3 7ST

Swallows and Amazons (novel) copyright © 1930 The Estate of Arthur Ransome
Swallows and Amazons (adaptation) copyright © 2011 Helen Edmundson and Neil Hannon

Helen Edmundson and Neil Hannon have asserted their right to be identified as the adapters of this work

Cover image by Quinton Winter (www.quintonwinter.com)
Cover design by Ned Hoste, 2H

Typeset by Nick Hern Books, London
Printed and bound in Great Britain by Mimeo Ltd, Cambridgeshire PE29 6XX

A CIP catalogue record for this book is available from the British Library

ISBN 978 1 84842 237 7

Production Note

Imagination is at the very centre of *Swallows and Amazons*. The children in the story are given the freedom to act out an ambitious, enthralling, imaginative game. And that proved to be the key to this adaptation, and to the staging of it. No need for real boats on real water, no need for owls and cormorants, no need, even, for children (they were played by adults in the first production, although I would love to see children perform it). If the imaginative world is established from the start, the audience will understand and enjoy the fact that boxes can become boats, and feather dusters can become parrots. The only required truth is in the emotions of the Swallows and the Amazons, as they negotiate their way through this extraordinary adventure.

Helen Edmundson

This stage adaptation of *Swallows and Amazons* was first performed at the Bristol Old Vic on 1 December 2010, with the following cast:

NANCY BLACKETT	Celia Adams
PEGGY BLACKETT	Amy Booth-Steel
SUSAN WALKER	Rosalie Craig
TITTY WALKER	Akiya Henry
JOHN WALKER	Stuart McLoughlin
ROGER WALKER	Stewart Wright
MOTHER	Alice Barclay
MR JACKSON	Trevor Michael Georges
POLICEMAN	Fionn Gill
OLD BILLY	Pieter Lawman
CAPTAIN FLINT	Richard Standing
PIRATE	Kyra Williams

Adapter	Helen Edmundson
Composer	Neil Hannon
Director	Tom Morris
Director of Movement	Toby Sedgwick
Set and Costume Designer	Robert Innes Hopkins
Musical Supervision/Arrangements/ Orchestrations	Sam Kenyon
Lighting Designer	James Farncombe
Sound Designer	Jason Barnes
Additional Arrangements	Andrew Skeet
Additional Musical Material	Sam Kenyon
Co-Costume Designer	Liesel Corp
Casting Director	Alison Chard

The National Theatre in association with the Children's Touring
Partnership presented the Bristol Old Vic production of
Swallows and Amazons at the Vaudeville Theatre in London's
West End, on 15 December 2011, with the following cast:

NANCY BLACKETT	Celia Adams
TITTY WALKER	Akiya Henry
JOHN WALKER	Richard Holt
SUSAN WALKER	Katie Moore
PEGGY BLACKETT	Sophie Waller
ROGER WALKER	Stewart Wright
CAPTAIN FLINT	Greg Barnett
FATHER/YOUNG BILLY	Neal Craig
MR JACKSON/PIRATE	Adrian Garratt
PIRATE	Alison George
MOTHER	Hilary Tones
POLICEMAN/OLD BILLY	Jon Trenchard
	Francesca Bradley

Adapter	Helen Edmundson
Composer	Neil Hannon
Director	Tom Morris
Director of Movement	Toby Sedgwick
Set and Costume Designer	Robert Innes Hopkins
Musical Supervision/Arrangements/	Sam Kenyon
Orchestrations	
Lighting Designer	James Farncombe
Sound Designer	Jason Barnes
Additional Arrangements	Andrew Skeet
Additional Musical Material	Sam Kenyon
Co-Costume Designer	Liesel Corp
Casting Director	Alison Chard

The production subsequently toured to Chichester Festival Theatre;
Festival Theatre Edinburgh; Theatre Royal, Nottingham; Belgrade
Theatre, Coventry; Wycombe Swan Theatre, High Wycombe; Malvern
Festival Theatre; Civic Theatre, Darlington; West Yorkshire Playhouse;
Liverpool Playhouse; Marlowe Theatre, Canterbury; Lyceum Theatre,
Sheffield; Cambridge Arts Theatre; Grand Theatre, Wolverhampton;
Theatre Royal Plymouth and New Theatre, Cardiff.

Characters

Swallows
TITTY WALKER
ROGER WALKER
JOHN WALKER
SUSAN WALKER

Amazons
NANCY BLACKETT
PEGGY BLACKETT

Grown-ups
MOTHER
MR JACKSON
CAPTAIN FLINT
CHARCOAL BURNER 1
CHARCOAL BURNER 2
PIRATE 1
PIRATE 2
POLICEMAN

This text went to press before the end of rehearsals and so may differ slightly from the play as performed.

ACT ONE

Scene One

The attic of an old house. A very old lady (TITTY), *enters. She is carrying a feather duster in her hand. She looks about her. She has not been up here for a long time, and, slowly, she reacquaints herself with her old possessions: a cabin trunk, an old-fashioned typewriter, a stuffed parrot, a whistling kettle, pots and pans, blankets. She sits down and takes up an old photograph album. She blows the dust from the cover and opens it. As she turns the pages, the photographs she is looking at come to life. There are two of young men in Naval uniform* (JOHN *and* ROGER). *One is of a very smartly dressed, intellectual-looking lady* (SUSAN). *The last is of a kind-looking lady, arm in arm with a Naval Commander* (MOTHER *and Father*). TITTY *smiles.*

Suddenly the feather duster sits up and squawks. TITTY *stares at it in astonishment, then remembers.*

TITTY. Polly?

The duster is transformed into a parrot. It squawks again, and flies to her. It lands on her hand.

Polly.

She strokes its feathers. After a moment, TITTY *begins to sing.*

Song – 'Like Robinson Crusoe'

Since I was three I've longed to be like Robinson Crusoe,
Making my home all on my own like Robinson Crusoe,
This is my own Pacific isle, no one around for miles and
    miles,
It's rather frightening,
One little wave follows another,
One tiny bird dives for its supper,

One buzzing bee flies through the heather,
One perfect day to last for ever.

Polly flies off. In her mind, TITTY *returns to the Peak in Darien – the promontory in the Lake District from where she and her siblings liked to gaze out across the lake to the island.*

(*Speaking*.) Look at it. A desert island. Waiting for us to discover it.

A little boy (ROGER) *runs in. He has a telegram in his hand. He runs round and round the stage, imitating a sailboat.*

ROGER. Dispatches! Dispatches!

TITTY. Roger? Roger!

ROGER. Dispatches! Dispatches!

Scene Two

Summer 1929. The peak of a hill in the Lake District (Peak in Darien). TITTY *is suddenly a girl again. Beside her is her brother,* JOHN, *who is stoking a small fire. Her sister,* SUSAN, *is sitting on a rock making marmalade sandwiches.* TITTY *springs to her feet as* ROGER *runs up.*

ROGER. Dispatches! Dispatches!

TITTY (*jumping up*). The telegram from Daddy!

SUSAN. At last.

ROGER *reaches them.*

TITTY. What does it say?

ROGER. Mother hasn't opened it. She says John should.

JOHN *takes it and opens it quickly. He reads and smiles.*

SUSAN. Well?

TITTY. What?

ROGER. What does it say?

SUSAN. Read it aloud.

JOHN. It says, 'Better drowned than duffers if not duffers won't drown.'

ROGER. What?

TITTY. 'Better drowned than duffers if not duffers won't drown.'

JOHN. Good old Daddy.

SUSAN. But what does it mean?

TITTY. It means yes.

ROGER. Yes? For me too?

JOHN. All of us. We can all go and camp on the island.

ROGER. Hurrah, hurrah, hurrah! It's because I'm not the youngest any more.

JOHN. We can take *Swallow* and sail her across.

SUSAN. Can I see?

SUSAN *takes the telegram.*

ROGER. Fat Vicky can't come because she's the baby.

TITTY. Good old Daddy.

SUSAN. But what are 'duffers if not duffers'?

JOHN. It doesn't say that.

TITTY. It says that if we're duffers…

ROGER. What's a duffer?

SUSAN. A fool.

TITTY. Then we'd be better off drowned. Then it stops and starts again, and says that as we aren't duffers…

JOHN. '*If*'.

TITTY. Yes – *if* we aren't duffers we won't be drowned.

SUSAN. Daddy put that in to comfort Mother.

JOHN. This is marvellous. I thought it was never going to come. I thought it would be too late and the holiday would be over.

SUSAN. It did have to come all the way from Daddy's ship.

JOHN. Let's make Ship's Articles.

He sits, and takes a scrap of paper and a pencil from his pocket. He writes –

Sailing vessel – '*Swallow*'. Port – 'Jackson's Farm'. Owner…

SUSAN. Mr Jackson, the farmer, I suppose

JOHN. Master – John Walker, aged twelve. Mate?

SUSAN. Susan Walker, aged eleven.

JOHN. Able Seaman?

TITTY. Titty Walker, aged nine.

JOHN. Ship's Boy?

ROGER. Me! Roger Walker, aged nearly eight.

JOHN. Aged seven.

Now, you all have to sign opposite your names.

ROGER. Can we go now?

SUSAN. Of course we can't go now. A lot of preparations must be made for a voyage.

TITTY. But if we hurry…

JOHN. We can go tomorrow – if there's a wind.

SUSAN. There's no wind at all today.

JOHN. If there's no wind we won't be able to sail, and we'll have to wait.

ROGER. Wait?

TITTY. But we can't wait any longer. (*Gazing out across the lake to the island.*) Look at it. Our island.

SUSAN. We've waited for three weeks already. A day or two more won't do any harm.

TITTY. We'll have to make the wind come. We'll have to whistle for it.

ROGER. But I can't whistle. You know I can't.

TITTY. We'll have to try. We'll all have to try.

Song – 'Whistle for a Wind'

SWALLOWS.
> Not a whisper in the beech trees,
> Not a ripple on the lake,
> The wind has gone to sleep, we've
> Got to whistle her awake.
> Whistle for a wind, whistle for a wind,
> Then and only then can it begin.

MOTHER *enters*.

MOTHER (*speaking*). Come on, time for bed!

Scene Three

The bedroom at the farmhouse on Jackson's Farm. MOTHER, holding Fat Vicky under her arm, settles them all into bed. The SWALLOWS *continue to sing.*

SWALLOWS.
> All of us are thirsting,
> For what tomorrow holds,
> But we are at the mercy,
> Of things we can't control,
> Let's whistle for a wind, whistle for a wind,
> Then and only then can we begin.

MOTHER (*speaking*). Goodnight, John.

JOHN. Goodnight.

MOTHER. A big day tomorrow. Your maiden voyage as Captain.

JOHN. Yes.

MOTHER. Quite a thing, being responsible for a crew.

JOHN. I think I'm up to it.

MOTHER. I'm sure you are. I'm sure you'll make Daddy proud. (*Kisses* JOHN.)

ROGER. I'm going to learn to swim on the island.

MOTHER. That's a very good idea. But only go in the water if one of the others is with you.

ROGER. I can nearly swim.

MOTHER. I know. And if you manage to swim properly, without your foot on the bottom, I shall give you a penknife of your own.

ROGER. Like John's? With a pearly handle?

MOTHER. Yes. Just like John's.

ROGER. Thanks! I'm definitely going to swim.

MOTHER (*kissing him*). Goodnight, darling.

TITTY (*singing*).
    I want to be a pirate, the terror of the seas.

SUSAN.
    I want to build a fireplace and make us all some tea.

JOHN.
    I'll be *Swallow*'s captain.

SUSAN, TITTY *and* ROGER.
    And we her willing crew.

SUSAN.
    First Mate.

TITTY.
    Able Seaman.

ROGER.
    And I am coming too!

MOTHER (*speaking*). Get back in your beds.

TITTY. You will come and wave us off, won't you?

MOTHER. Of course.

TITTY. You can be Queen Isabella waving goodbye to the Spanish Armada. And John can be Stout Cortez and we'll be the conquistadors.

MOTHER. And you can bring me back some treasure.

TITTY. Pirate treasure buried hundreds of years ago!

MOTHER. I'll ask the farm opposite the island if they'll give you milk and bread every day.

SUSAN. And eggs too. I'm best at buttered eggs.

MOTHER. Just be sure to clean out the milk can very thoroughly. We don't want any sickness in the crew.

SUSAN. Or scurvy.

TITTY. You don't mind us all going, do you? And leaving you, I mean?

SUSAN. At least you'll have Vicky.

TITTY. But Vicky can't chat.

SUSAN. She says more than Mr Jackson.

TITTY. I'll miss our chats.

MOTHER. So will I.

ROGER. Is that the wind?

They all sing.

ALL.
>Like another lonely planet,
>Like a strange and distant star,
>Stretch out, you can almost touch it,
>So near but yet so far.
>Whistle for a wind, whistle for a wind,
>Then and only then can it begin,
>Then and only then can it begin.

ROGER (*speaking*). Goodnight for tonight. And goodnight for tomorrow night. And goodnight for the next night, and the next night.

MOTHER. Sleep!

MOTHER *leaves, putting the light out as she does so.* ROGER *manages to whistle.*

ROGER. I whistled!

ALL. Go to sleep, Roger!

The sun sets. The CHILDREN *settle down to sleep. Night falls and it grows completely dark. The faintest whisper of a wind begins to blow the curtain. Gradually it grows. Trees begin to sway, and things begin to blow about. At last the wind fills the whole auditorium so that the audience feels it too.*

Scene Four

The sun comes out. The four CHILDREN *rush outside and spin round and round in the wind, laughing and whooping for joy.*

ROGER. It worked! The whistling worked!

SUSAN. What sort of wind is it, John?

JOHN (*holding his finger up*). North-westerly.

TITTY. Is that good?

JOHN. It will do us nicely.

ROGER. Can we go? Can we go?

JOHN. Wait, Roger. Where's that list, Mister Mate? Let's start packing.

SUSAN. Aye, aye, Cap'n!

Song – 'Packing'

A big tin box of books and writing paper.

JOHN.
A small aneroid barometer.

SUSAN.
And other things that need to be kept dry.

TITTY.
Like nightclothes.

JOHN.
I won it as a prize at school…

ROGER (*speaking, over the music*). Hurry up! The wind's getting stronger!

SUSAN (*singing*).
Three biscuit tins with bread and tea and sugar.

TITTY.
Salt and bread, and lots and lots of eggs – separately wrapped for fear of smashes.

SUSAN.
A frying pan, a saucepan and a kettle.

JOHN *and* ROGER.
Jugs and plates and spoons and forks and knives.

SUSAN.
Two groundsheets with tents wrapped up inside.

TITTY.
A seed cake.

JOHN *and* ROGER.
A long coil of stout grass rope.

TITTY.
Two sacks stuffed with blankets and rugs.

SUSAN.
Tins of corned beef. Where's the corned beef?

JOHN (*speaking*). Right, crew, let's get this down to the boathouse.

They head off, continuing to check the list as they go.

Scene Five

They reach the boathouse. The CHILDREN *open the doors.*

JOHN. I'll bring her out.

SUSAN. I'll undo the painter.

> (*Singing.*)
> A piece of chalk, a plaster and some candles.

TITTY (*speaking*). Is her sail up?

SUSAN. No. It's rolled up inside.

JOHN (*singing*).
> The fishing rod I got at Christmas time.

SUSAN (*speaking*). And her mast is there. And her boom.

ROGER. Put it up! Put it up!

> JOHN *brings* Swallow *out.* JOHN *and* SUSAN *put the mast up and fix the boom. They stare at her in admiration.*

SWALLOWS (*singing*).
> Swallow, we've yearned so long for this day to arrive.

> TITTY *pulls something from her pocket. It is a little flag, with a blue swallow on it. She hoists it to the top of the mast.*

TITTY (*speaking*). There – a beautiful boat deserves a beautiful flag.

SWALLOWS (*singing*).
> And now it has finally come,
> And the adventure's begun.

> MOTHER *arrives with Fat Vicky and* MR JACKSON, *who is pulling a wheelbarrow loaded with lots of other essentials.*

MOTHER (*speaking*). That is a beautiful flag.

TITTY (*bowing*). Your Majesty. I made it yesterday out of scraps. It's sewn not glued.

MOTHER. Even better.

ROGER. Hello, Mr Jackson. Isn't she a fine boat?

JACKSON. Aye.

SUSAN (*singing*).
    A frying pan, a saucepan,
    There's the tins of corned beef, tins of sardines.

SUSAN *and* JOHN.
    I think we have all that we need.

TITTY (*speaking*). Goodbye, Queen Isabella.

MOTHER. Goodbye, loyal subjects.

ROGER. Goodbye, Fat Vicky! Goodbye, Mr Jackson!

The SWALLOWS *climb into the boat.* MOTHER *undoes the painter. They push off.*

SWALLOWS (*singing*).
    Farewell and adieu to you, fair Spanish ladies,
    Adieu and farewell to you, ladies of Spain…

MOTHER (*speaking*). Keep the oil away from the tents!

SWALLOWS (*singing*).
    For we're under orders to sail for old England,
    And we'll never see all you ladies again…

MOTHER (*speaking*). Don't forget to row for supplies!

SWALLOWS (*singing*).
    We'll rant and we'll roar just like true British sailors,
    We'll range and we'll roam over all the salt seas…

MOTHER (*speaking*). Leave word that you're all right!
    Farewell, my brave explorers!

SWALLOWS (*singing*).
    Until we strike sounding for the English Channel,
    From Ushant to Scilly 'tis thirty-five leagues…

ROGER (*speaking*). Here it is! Here it is!

Song – 'Swallow'

SWALLOWS.
>Hoist up the mainsail, haul in the anchor,
>Make fast the halyard, let go the painter,
>It's time to put to sea,
>And set the *Swallow* free.

ROGER (*speaking*). Look! The wind! The wind is in the sail!

SWALLOWS (*singing*).
>*Swallow*, the wind blows fair in the east,
>Feel the breeze,
>Show them that you're the best boat ever to be set afloat,
>Show them, *Swallow*.

JOHN (*speaking*). Ready about!

SWALLOWS (*singing*).
>*Swallow*, I almost think you're alive sometimes,
>When I am lost and confused,
>You seem to know what to do,
>Don't you, *Swallow*.

Scene Six

Swallow *is sailing swiftly towards the island*.

ROGER (*waving*). Bye, bye, Peak of Darien! Goodbye, Mr Jackson's cows!

TITTY. The lake is a desolate ocean, and we're the first people to cross it.

ROGER (*taking out a chunk of bread*). Time for refreshments.

SUSAN. Where did you get that?

ROGER. Breakfast. I saved it in my sock. Want some?

SUSAN. No, thank you.

JOHN. Keep a good lookout, Ship's Boy.

ROGER. Aye, aye. What for?

TITTY. Everything.

JOHN. Enemy vessels.

TITTY. Barbarians.

SUSAN. Are we all right about gybing, Captain? We don't want any bashed heads.

JOHN. Look at the flag – it's blowing well over on the same side as the sail. There's no fear of a gybe as long as it's doing that.

ROGER. You can see the whole world in one go.

SUSAN. Everything looks tiny.

We see MOTHER, *waving*.

TITTY. Goodbye, Queen Isabella!

SUSAN. There's smoke in the woods on that shore across there. It must be the charcoal burners.

TITTY. What do charcoal burners do?

SUSAN. Burn charcoal, I suppose. Mother says they're very mysterious and quiet.

TITTY. Like hermits.

ROGER. Look! I mean, ship ahoy! At least, I think it's a ship.

Some way ahead of them, they can see a houseboat.

TITTY. Oh, yes. How funny it is.

JOHN. It's a houseboat.

TITTY. What's a houseboat?

JOHN. It's a boat used instead of a house. People live on them all year round.

SUSAN. And have post delivered and everything.

ROGER. There's a man on deck!

TITTY. Barbarian ahoy!

SUSAN. Oh, yes. He's writing.

JOHN. Where?

> JOHN *steers off-course and* Swallow *lurches slightly.*

SUSAN. Look what you're doing, John!

JOHN. Oh!

> *The boom is about to swing over, but* JOHN *puts the helm down just in time.*

Sorry, crew.

TITTY. I wonder if he lives there on his own.

SUSAN. Perhaps his wife is cooking in the cabin.

> ROGER *spots a little brass cannon on the deck.*

ROGER. He's got a cannon!

SUSAN. Where?

ROGER. There.

SUSAN. Oh, yes.

TITTY. He's not just a barbarian: he must be a pirate. A retired pirate.

SUSAN. Or a writer – every writer should have a cannon.

> *There is a loud squawk, and they suddenly see a parrot on a perch close to the man.*

ROGER. A parrot! He's got a parrot!

TITTY. That settles it. He is a pirate!

> *They sail on.*

JOHN. Ready about, Lee-O!

> *They pass a small, bare island.*

Look at that island.

SUSAN. Oh, yes. We couldn't see that from Darien.

TITTY. How strange and eerie.

ROGER. What are those black shapes in the trees?

SUSAN. I can't tell.

JOHN. They're cormorants!

SUSAN. Yes!

TITTY. No, no. They're not cormorants. They're harpies.

ROGER. What are harpies?

TITTY. They terrorise all sailors who pass too near.

ROGER. What do they do?

TITTY. They swoop down and peck their heads off.

Unseen by ROGER, *a cormorant has flown down over the boat. It snatches the bread from his hand.*

ROGER. Hey, don't take my… (*Sees the cormorant.*) Ah! Ah!

JOHN. Keep still, Roger!

SUSAN. Don't fuss, Roger!

ROGER. But… But it got my bread!

TITTY. Lucky it was only your bread.

SUSAN. There it goes. Back to its nest.

JOHN. We'll have to go back there. Explore the terrain and chart it.

TITTY. The Island of the Harpies.

JOHN. Cormorant Island.

ROGER. I'm never going there! Horrible bird! I'm never ever ever going there.

SUSAN. It's just a bird, Roger.

ROGER. Never ever. Ever.

JOHN. Here it is! Here's our island! Look out for a good landing place, everyone!

TITTY. And look out for barbarians. We don't know if it's uninhabited.

JOHN. I'll sail all the way round it, so we can choose the best place.

They start to sail around the island. They all duck as the boom swings.

ROGER. Rocks ahead!

JOHN. I'll come a bit further out. Ready to gybe. Gybe-O!

SUSAN *hauls in the sheet as fast as she can.* JOHN *puts the helm up.* Swallow *turns and the boom swings.*

That bay looks like the only place. It's exposed, but it will have to do. Stand by to take in sail! Lower away!

SUSAN *takes down the sail using the halyard.*

SUSAN. Grab the yard, Roger!

ROGER *does so. They put sail and yard down in the boat.*

TITTY. Rock on the starboard bow!

JOHN *shifts the tiller.*

JOHN. She's coming in nicely.

SUSAN. I'll move to the stern.

SUSAN *moves forward.*

JOHN. Any moment... any moment... Now!

There is a gentle grumble and a scrunch as Swallow*'s nose meets the pebbly beach.* ROGER *jumps out first with the painter. He secures it. They all carry something off the boat and put it down on the island.*

ROGER. We're here!

Scene Seven

TITTY. Our own desert island.

SUSAN. A new continent.

ROGER. We could be anywhere.

They begin to explore the island.

Song – 'The Conquering Heroes'

TITTY.

When Stout Cortez was staring out over the Pacific,
I wonder what he thought about?

JOHN.

He thought about, without a doubt, whether there'd be
perch or trout,
Cortez loved his fishing.

TITTY (*speaking*). I'm Charles Darwin and I'm looking for
giant tortoises.

JOHN. I'm Blériot flying the Channel.

SUSAN. I'm Mrs Beeton and I'm looking for wild parsley.

ROGER. I'm Mowgli and I'm getting suckled by wolves.

ALL. No, Roger.

SUSAN (*singing*).

I am Marco Polo, let me tell you where we are,
We are on the Silk Road from China to Milan.

JOHN.

I'm Christopher Columbus and I've just found America.

SUSAN.

Christopher, well done, but weren't you looking for
Japan?

SWALLOWS.
> We are conquering heroes, we are famous explorers,
> We are mighty conquistadors lusting for gold and war,
> Every stream is a river, every tree is is a forest,
> Every rock is a mountain range, new and strange,
> Hereby claimed by the Swallows.

JOHN is standing in a clearing near the large pine tree. There is a spot in the middle of the space, where the turf has been scraped away and someone has built a primitive fireplace. Next to it is a pile of neat, dry sticks. The others run up.

JOHN (*speaking*). Look.

TITTY. Barbarians!

JOHN. Very clever barbarians. This is an excellent fireplace, and this is a great spot for a camp.

SUSAN (*looking at the woodpile*). And they're very well prepared too.

TITTY. They must be coming back.

ROGER. Perhaps they're still here and they're watching us right now.

JOHN. We must spread out and search. Every inch of the island. Whistle, or give the secret signal if you find anything.

ROGER. What's the secret signal?

SUSAN. Hoot like an owl.

ROGER. Oh, yes. Twit-twhoo!

> (*Singing, stealthily.*)
> We are conquering heroes, we are famous explorers,
> We are mighty conquistadors lusting for gold and war,
> Every stream is a river…

JOHN (*speaking*). Hoot!

SUSAN. What is it?

TITTY. We're coming!

ROGER. Is it barbarians?

JOHN. No. I declare this territory entirely free of barbarians.
But look!

They do so. It is a hidden harbour.

SUSAN. It's completely hidden by the rocks!

TITTY. It's just right for escaping to. Or making a quick
getaway.

JOHN. It's the perfect harbour for *Swallow*!

SWALLOWS (*singing*).
    Every stream is a river, every tree is a forest,
    Every rock is a mountain range, new and strange,
    Hereby claimed by the Swallows.

*Suddenly the peace is shattered by a very loud bang, which
seems to come from the lake.*

JOHN (*speaking*). What on earth…?

SUSAN. What was that?

TITTY. It wasn't on the island.

ROGER. It sounded like a gun!

*They all rush to the lookout point. JOHN scans the horizon
with his telescope.*

JOHN. There's smoke over there – a big cloud of it. Near the
houseboat.

TITTY. The cannon! It must have been the cannon!

JOHN. It's possible.

ROGER. The pirate!

SUSAN. But…

JOHN. Just a minute… ship ahoy!

TITTY. Oh, yes. I see it.

SUSAN. There are two boys in her.

JOHN. Girls.

TITTY. Girls?

JOHN. Girls with red caps, and they're coming right this way.

TITTY. Can I see? (*Takes the telescope*.) She's sailing close to the wind.

JOHN. She must have a centreboard. You can do that with a centreboard.

SUSAN. Can I see? (*Takes the telescope*.) They're dressed exactly alike.

ROGER. Can I see?

JOHN. No. Get down, everyone. They could be enemies.

They all drop down. JOHN *peers over a rock*.

I can read the boat's name – '*Am – a – zon*'. *Amazon*.

TITTY. What are they doing now?

SUSAN (*peering over*). They're really close.

ROGER. Can I…?

TITTY. Stay down, Roger.

JOHN. They're fixing something to the mast… they're hoisting a flag… Oh!

TITTY (*peering over*). What? Oh!

SUSAN *and* ROGER (*peering over*). Oh!

TITTY. It is. It is.

ROGER. It's the Jolly Roger.

TITTY. Pirates!

JOHN. Stay down.

ROGER. Are they going to land?

SUSAN. No. They're turning back.

TITTY. They're hauling down the flag.

JOHN. They must have hoisted it just for us. To show us.

SUSAN. To warn us. That's what it felt like.

TITTY. Let's go after them.

ROGER. Let's see where they go.

JOHN. I'm with you there. Come on!

SUSAN. But we've only just got here.

JOHN. It doesn't matter.

SUSAN. But we haven't had lunch!

JOHN. Come on, Susan!

They all rush off.

Scene Eight

Swallow *sails off after the* Amazon.

Song – 'Fighting Swallow'

SWALLOWS.
> *Swallow*, the fastest ship under the sun,
> Bar none,
> Carry us over the waves to the adventure we crave,
> Gybe-O, *Swallow*,
> *Swallow*, there's not a moment to lose,
> Time to prove,
> You have the speed to outrun practically anyone,
> Come on, *Swallow*.
>
> Load up the cannon, powder the musket,
> Steel up the sinews, sharpen the cutlass,
> We'll send our enemies to the bottom of the sea.

JOHN (*speaking*). She's heading for Houseboat Bay.

TITTY. They must be part of the Houseboat Man Pirate's crew.
I'm sure it was him who fired the cannon.

ROGER. Don't go near the Harpy Island.

JOHN. She's not stopping. She's gone straight past. They
certainly know how to steer.

TITTY. She's getting away!

ROGER. Past the Peak of Darien.

SUSAN. She must be going to the town.

JOHN. Rio – not the town.

SUSAN. She must be going to Rio.

ROGER. Look! Look at the Houseboat Man Pirate!

The Houseboat Man is shaking his fist at them.

TITTY. He's very angry.

SUSAN. How rude.

ROGER *shakes his fist back.*

Don't, Roger.

JOHN. They'll have lost the wind on the other side of Darien. I
think we'll be able to spot them once we get round there.

ROGER. There's Holly Howe. Hello, Mother! Hello, Fat Vicky!

SUSAN. There's Mr Jackson with his cows.

TITTY. They don't even know that we're in desperate pursuit of
a pirate ship.

JOHN. Stand by, crew. We're coming round the Peak. Sing out
if you spot her!

They round the Peak in Darien.

SUSAN. There are too many boats in Rio Bay.

ROGER. Sail ho!

SUSAN. Where? (*Takes the telescope*.) He's right. It's her.

ROGER. She's miles away.

JOHN. She's going round the headland.

TITTY. Gone. What shall we do now?

ROGER. Go after her. And be quicker this time.

SUSAN. I don't know… It's an awfully long way and we haven't had lunch.

JOHN. She might be trying to draw us away from the island. If we sail down there and she comes out again, we might have to race her back.

SUSAN. I think we should go back.

ROGER. But we're in a desperate pursuit!

JOHN. No, Susan's right. We'll make camp and have lunch. And then I'll row to Dickson's Farm and leave word for Mother that we're all right.

TITTY. We said we'd do that every day.

JOHN. Stand by, crew. Ready about! Gybe-O!

Scene Nine

Three hours later. The tents are up. SUSAN *is getting a fire going.* ROGER *and* TITTY *are in the lake, playing.*

SUSAN (*calling*). No further out than that, Roger!

TITTY. Are you swimming, Roger?

ROGER. Yes.

TITTY (*to* ROGER). Let's be pearl divers.

ROGER. I can't go upside down.

TITTY. Watch.

She dives down and wiggles her feet in the air. She comes up with a white pebble.

ROGER. A beauty!

TITTY. Let's show Susan.

They come out of the lake. TITTY is first. ROGER winces as he crosses the shingle in bare feet.

I found a pearl.

ROGER. Oo, ah. Oo, ah.

SUSAN. That's a very good pearl. Well done, Titty.

TITTY. No sign of the pirates?

SUSAN. I'm afraid not.

TITTY. I don't suppose we'll ever see them again.

SUSAN. Did you swim, Ship's Boy?

ROGER. Yes.

SUSAN. Without a foot on the bottom?

ROGER. No. But I changed foot quite a lot. Look at that fire!

SUSAN. I think it's finally taken.

TITTY. It looks like a real camp now.

ROGER. Can we have buttered eggs for tea?

SUSAN. Yes.

ROGER. Hurrah!

SUSAN. As long as the fire stays in. We'll eat out of the common dish. Egg's awful stuff for sticking to plates.

TITTY. Here's John coming back! Ahoy there!

TITTY and ROGER help pull Swallow *in. JOHN disembarks.*

Did you bring dispatches?

ROGER. Did you bring cake?

JOHN. I'm afraid that'll have to wait. I'm calling a council.

ROGER. Council! Council, everyone!

SUSAN. Has something happened?

ROGER. Sit down, everyone!

They do so.

JOHN. It seems we have an enemy.

TITTY. The pirates?

ROGER. The harpy?

SUSAN. Hush.

JOHN. The man who owns the houseboat has been telling the
barbarians that we've been meddling with his boat.

TITTY. What? We've never touched it.

JOHN. He thinks we have. He's trying to turn the barbarians
against us and he says we shouldn't be allowed to camp on
the island. I don't know why, but he hates us.

SUSAN. So he was shaking his fist at us.

TITTY. I knew he was a bad old pirate. He has a secret. They all
have.

SUSAN. Perhaps this is his island. Perhaps he...

*At that moment, something flies through the air and hits the
kettle with a loud ping. It is an arrow, with a green feather
sticking out of it.*

JOHN. Look out, everyone!

TITTY. Ah! An arrow!

ROGER. Indians!

TITTY. A parrot feather!

SUSAN. A parrot feather?

TITTY. It's him! It must be him!

ROGER *goes to pick it up.*

Don't touch the point, it might be poisoned!

JOHN. Hush, all of you. Listen…

The sharp crack of a dry stick is heard coming from the middle of the island.

SUSAN (*whispering*). He's here.

JOHN. We must scout. Spread out. Titty, you keep Roger with you.

ROGER. I can go on my own. I'm not a baby. Fat Vicky's the…

SUSAN. Be quiet, Roger.

JOHN. Hoot like an owl if you see anything

ALL. Aye, aye.

They split up and go different ways. But they haven't gone ten yards when –

JOHN. *Swallow*! *Swallow*'s gone!

They all rush to the beach.

ROGER. Oh, no!

SUSAN. He can't have taken her! He wouldn't dare, would he?

JOHN. But he has! Spread out again. This is war. Comb every inch of the island.

They spread out again.

TITTY. Roger, have you got a weapon?

ROGER. No. Have you?

TITTY. Yes. I've got two sticks – I mean, pikes. You'd better have one.

She throws him one. He catches it.

ROGER. Titty?

TITTY. Yes?

ROGER. If anything happens to me, and I don't come through
this...

SUSAN suddenly sounds a loud hoot.

SUSAN. HOOT!

TITTY. That's the Mate! Come on.

The SWALLOWS *converge on* SUSAN, *who is examining a
patch of grass.*

SUSAN. Someone's been here! Look how flat the grass is.

ROGER (*spotting something*). And look!

He picks up a clasp knife from the floor.

A clasp knife. A beauty. He must have dropped it. Finders
keepers.

SUSAN. Don't be silly, Roger.

JOHN. He can't be far. He can't have taken *Swallow* out to sea
or we would have seen her. He must...

There are sudden sounds of a terrifying chanting.

TITTY. What's that?

JOHN. The camp!

They charge back to the camp. The chanting gets louder.

Flat on your faces!

*They throw themselves to the ground. An arrow whistles over
their heads. They dare to look up again.*

ROGER. Do you see what I see?

*A tall stick has been driven into the ground in the middle of
the camp. There is a Jolly Roger flying from it.*

TITTY. Pirates!

Then they see the two girls from Amazon (NANCY *and*
PEGGY) *in their tents and aiming arrows at them.*

JOHN. In our camp!

ROGER. Take them prisoner!

TITTY. We outnumber them!

NANCY. This means war!

> *The* AMAZONS *begin to sing, whilst performing a terrifying war dance.*

Song – 'The Amazon Pirates'

AMAZONS (*chanting*).
> Amazons, Amazons, Amazons, Amazons…
> THIS MEANS WAR!

> (*Singing.*)
> Raised by our mama on the banks of the Amazon Delta,
> With only the clouds and a four-bedroom house for shelter,
> We took to the lake like a duckling takes to water,
> Then we took to a life of crime and mindless slaughter,
> We're the Amazon Pirates, the Amazon Pirates,
> The Amazon Pirates, the Amazon Pirates…

> Amazons, Amazons, Amazons, Amazons…
> THIS MEANS WAR!

JOHN.
> Parley, parley?
> Maybe we can talk this through?

AMAZONS.
> We swash our buckles and we go looking for trouble on
>   the high seas,
> In the darkness we go by the stars.

PEGGY.
> I'm a Leo.

NANCY.
> I'm a Pisces.

AMAZONS.
> When we go into battle we scream and rattle our sabres,
> But we're banned from fighting on land cos it frightens
>   the neighbours,
> We're the Amazon Pirates, the Amazon Pirates…

JOHN.
> Parley, parley, maybe we can talk this through,
> Parley, parley, talk with me, I'll talk with you.

PEGGY (*speaking, to* NANCY). What does he mean, 'Parley'?

Song – 'Parley'

JOHN.
> When captains see the slightest hope of stopping a
>   bloodbath, they
> Sheathe their weapons and invoke,
> The ancient right of parley.

ROGER.
> A parley, Titty, let's do that,
> It sounds awfully exciting.

TITTY.
> It's where we all sit round and chat,
> It's not as good as fighting.

JOHN *and* SUSAN.
> Parley, parley, maybe we can talk this through,
> Parley, parley, talk with me, I'll talk with you.

JOHN *takes a step towards the* AMAZONS.

JOHN (*speaking*). My name is John Walker, master of the ship *Swallow*. Who are you?

NANCY. I am Nancy Blackett, master and part-owner of the *Amazon*, the terror of the seas. This is Peggy Blackett, Mate.

PEGGY. Her real name is Ruth, but Uncle Jim said that Amazons were ruth-less, so we had to change it...

NANCY. Silence your scurvy tongue, you ninny, or I'll silence it for you!

(*Singing.*)
> We've got your ship and all your tents,
> We're older and we're bigger,
> We hold a pistol to your heads,
> I say we pull the trigger.

JOHN.

> A little older you my be,
> But we're in numbers greater,
> Let's have a parley first,
> And you can always kill us later.

JOHN, SUSAN *and* ROGER.

> Parley, parley, maybe we can talk this through,
> Parley, parley, talk with me, I'll talk with you.

TITTY (*speaking*). Where's your shipmate?

NANCY. What shipmate?

TITTY. The Houseboat Man Pirate, of course.

JOHN (*stepping in quickly*). Hand me that knife you found, Ship's Boy.

ROGER. What knife?

SUSAN. Don't be silly, Roger, give the Captain the knife.

> ROGER *does so, reluctantly.*

PEGGY. That's our knife! I must have dropped it.

NANCY. Peggy, you donkey!

PEGGY. That knife was given to us by Uncle Jim last year, for polishing the cannon on his houseboat.

TITTY. You mean, the Houseboat Man is your uncle?

PEGGY. Only sometimes.

TITTY. But if he's their uncle, they must be in league with him!

ROGER. Yes!

NANCY. We jolly well aren't.

PEGGY. He's our mortal enemy.

SUSAN. He's ours too.

PEGGY. What?

TITTY. But…

JOHN. Be quiet, Titty. All weapons down, everyone.

They all throw their weapons into a pile on the ground.

PEGGY (*singing*).
    It seems we're all on the same side.

SUSAN.
    So what's the good in fighting?

JOHN.
    Our purposes are intertwined.

ROGER.
    We're better off uniting.

TITTY.
    But no, they just invaded us,
    We must defend our island.

AMAZONS.
    Our island!

NANCY.
    This is our camp.

PEGGY.
    This is our island.

AMAZONS.
    We've been coming here for years.

NANCY.
    We marked the harbour.

PEGGY.
    Built the fireplace.

AMAZONS
    With our own blood, sweat and tears!

TITTY (*speaking*). Oh. Parley, then?

She throws her weapon down. The AMAZONS *begin to chant.*

SWALLOWS (*singing*).
    Parley, parley, maybe we can talk this through,
    Parley, parley, talk with me, I'll talk with you.

AMAZONS.
>Amazon parley, parley, parley,
>Amazon parley, parley, parley.

SWALLOWS.
>Parley, parley, maybe we can talk this through,
>Parley, parley, talk with me, I'll talk with you.

SUSAN (*speaking*). Hadn't we better sit down?

They do so.

JOHN. So, you claim this is your island?

NANCY. It is. We discovered it and we named it. What do you call it?

JOHN. We haven't given it a name yet.

PEGGY. It's called Wildcat Island. Uncle Jim called it that because it belongs to us and he says we're a pair of wildcats. Which we are.

JOHN. But it's our island now. It was uninhabited when we came, and we put our tents up here.

NANCY. And I say it's ours. And we'll defend it to the death.

ROGER. So will we.

SUSAN. Be quiet, Roger.

TITTY. And do you swear that the Houseboat Man Pirate isn't with you?

PEGGY. Of course he isn't.

JOHN. He didn't take *Swallow*?

NANCY. What? You think he would have the guts for that kind of fearsome piracy?

PEGGY. We took her.

ROGER. You? Give her back!

NANCY. We waited until you left the beach and then we struck. Quick as lightning!

SUSAN. I don't think you should have done that.

PEGGY. We were very careful with her. Mum always says we have to leave things as we find them because...

NANCY. Silence, you ninny.

JOHN. We'd like our ship back. Now, if possible.

NANCY. Oh, you'll get her back. When the time is right.

JOHN *and* SUSAN *exchange glances, uncertain how to deal with this.*

SUSAN. Would you like a glass of lemonade?

PEGGY. Lemonade?

TITTY. She means rum.

NANCY. All right. Don't mind if we do. Piracy is thirsty work.

SUSAN *goes to fetch the lemonade.*

TITTY. Is your Uncle Jim a retired pirate?

NANCY (*cautiously*). It's quite a good thing for him to be.

TITTY. And you are pirates too. I still think that's very suspicious.

NANCY. Pirates can be mortal enemies. He could be Captain Flint!

PEGGY. Yes.

ROGER. Who is Captain Flint?

TITTY. He was Captain of the pirate ship *Walrus*. He buried his treasure and slaughtered all six of his crew.

PEGGY. He cut their legs off!

NANCY. One day we'll make him walk the plank off the deck of his own ship.

ROGER. We'll help. Down with Captain Flint!

JOHN. He hates us. He's been stirring up the barbarians against us.

TITTY. But why is he your enemy? If he's your uncle?

PEGGY. Because he's ignoring us. Last summer he played with us… I mean, we saw him all the time. But this year someone's making him write a book and he keeps telling us to leave him alone.

ROGER. Charming.

PEGGY. We've offered to help and everything but he just tells us to go away.

SUSAN *is back with the lemonade and mugs.*

SUSAN. Here we are. Luckily Mother made us pack six mugs in case of breakages.

PEGGY. Our mugs aren't mugs, they're flagons.

TITTY. Yes. Ours are flagons too.

NANCY. So this morning, do you know what we did? We got an old firework out of the shed…

PEGGY. A gigantic banger.

NANCY. Then we lit it and threw it onto the roof of his boat.

SUSAN. Onto the roof of his boat? But…

PEGGY. And then we rowed away, really really fast.

NANCY. It couldn't have banged better.

ROGER. We heard it!

JOHN. We certainly did.

TITTY. We thought it was his cannon.

NANCY. I bet it made him savage.

JOHN. He was standing on deck shaking his fist when we were sailing up to Rio after you.

NANCY. Rio? Rio? We'll call it Rio if you like. It's a good name.

SUSAN. So is Wildcat Island.

NANCY. I propose an alliance.

ROGER. Good idea!

JOHN. What sort of alliance?

NANCY. An alliance against Captain Flint and all the grown-ups in the world.

ROGER. Barbarians, you mean.

TITTY. Except Queen Isabella.

NANCY. But we want the sort of alliance that will let us fight each other if we want to.

TITTY. That's a Treaty of Offence and Defence. There are lots of those in history books.

NANCY. Yes. Defence against our enemies, and all sorts of desperate battles between ourselves whenever we want. What do you say, Captain?

JOHN *glances at the others, then –*

JOHN. I agree.

NANCY. Spit and swear!

JOHN. What, sorry?

PEGGY. Spit and swear!

NANCY *spits on her hand and holds it out.* JOHN *glances at* SUSAN, *and then does the same. The others follow suit –* SUSAN *most reluctantly.*

NANCY. That seals it. Now we need to drink to it.

They raise their glasses.

PEGGY. Swallows and Amazons for ever and death to Uncle Jim!

NANCY. Captain Flint, you chump-headed galoot!

PEGGY. If I'm a chump-headed galoot, you're a pox-faced poltroon!

NANCY. And you're a scurvy swab!

PEGGY. And you're a smelly old pig!

SUSAN. Stop fighting.

PEGGY. Why?

SUSAN. Because it's just not a very nice thing to do.

PEGGY. But Amazons do whatever they want to.

ROGER. Crikey.

NANCY (*suddenly*). Swallows and Amazons for ever! And death to Captain Flint!

ALL. Swallows and Amazons for ever and death to Captain Flint!

NANCY. Now swig!

They all do so.

But look here, before we fight Captain Flint, let's try to capture each other's ships. Then the ship who wins shall be flagship for the great battle against Captain Flint, and her Captain will be Commodore of the whole fleet.

TITTY. I like that!

ROGER. Capture each other's ships?

NANCY. Yes. Beginning tomorrow. We only win if we get *Swallow* into our boathouse. And you win if you get *Amazon* into your harbour.

JOHN. Agreed.

ROGER. We'll win!

PEGGY. We'll see about that.

AMAZONS. Lolololololololololololo!

As they utter their war cry, the AMAZONS *head off. The others follow behind them, until only* ROGER *is left.*

ROGER. Crikey.

ROGER *runs after them.*

Scene Ten

Late the same day. It has grown dark.

JOHN. We're going to the harbour for a night council.

ROGER. Night council! Night council!

SUSAN. It's getting terribly late, John.

JOHN. This won't take too long. Get the hammer, Roger.

ROGER. Hammer!

    ROGER *picks up the hammer.*

SUSAN. We really ought to go to bed. Especially Roger.

ROGER. I'm not sleepy.

JOHN. I had an idea this afternoon. An important idea.

TITTY. To help us win the war?

    They all arrive in the harbour.

JOHN. Yes. Look at this white cross on the tree stump.

ROGER. Oh, yes.

SUSAN. I hadn't noticed that.

JOHN. The Amazons made it. And there's another mark, but it's a secret one.

TITTY. Where is it?

JOHN. It's this fork in the tree.

SUSAN. But what use is it all?

JOHN. It's extremely useful. If you're trying to navigate into the harbour, through the narrow channel, you look at those marks and steer so that one is always directly above the other. As long as you adjust your course all the time to keep them in line, you can scull straight in.

SUSAN. But that might only win us a minute or two of time.

JOHN. But that's not my idea. Listen: in real harbours, they turn these marks into lights at night, so that ships can navigate home in the dark. I remember Daddy telling me.

TITTY. That's clever.

JOHN. They call them 'leading lights'. And we're going to do the same with these. Watch…

He hammers a nail into the middle of the white cross on the tree stump.

Pass me a lantern, Susan.

She does so. He fixes it to the nail. They go to the forked tree.

And now I'll fix one here – it'll have to be a little below the fork so that Titty can reach it. But as long as it's directly in line, it will be all right. Stretch up, Titty, and let's see how high it can go.

ROGER. But what about me? I have to reach it.

SUSAN. No you don't. You're not allowed to use matches, so you'll never be lighting it.

ROGER (*indignant*). Huh!

JOHN. Can you open the lantern, and reach inside?

TITTY. Yes. Just.

JOHN. Good. Lantern, Susan. (*Fixes the lantern in place.*) Now, all come down to the edge of the water. Squat down and imagine you're in *Swallow*. Do you see? If you keep them directly above one another, you know you're on a safe course.

TITTY (*moving her head from left to right*). It works!

SUSAN. But how will it help us to win the war?

JOHN. Because it's the one thing the Amazons think we can't do. They think we wouldn't attack in the dark because we wouldn't be able to get back to our harbour.

TITTY. But now we can.

ROGER. So let's go now! Let's take *Amazon*!

SUSAN. The only place you're going now is bed.

JOHN. And besides, that would be cheating. The war doesn't start till tomorrow. But we're going to win. I promise you that.

TITTY. I can't wait.

SUSAN. Come on now. Bring the lanterns. Let's go and get some sleep. We'll be up with the birds in the morning.

They start to head back, but JOHN *doesn't move and* SUSAN *goes to him.*

John? Don't you think it's too dangerous? To be out on the lake in the dark?

JOHN. Why? We'll have the compass. We have to win, Susan. That Amazon Captain is a bit too big for her boots. We have to win.

Scene Eleven

In the camp. The SWALLOWS *settle in their tents.*

JOHN. Ready for lights-out, Mister Mate?

SUSAN. Aye, aye, sir.

The two lanterns are blown out. Only the glow of the fire remains.

After a moment, JOHN *comes out of the tent. He goes quietly to the edge of the lake and gazes out across the dark water.*

Song – 'Better Drowned Than Duffers'

JOHN.

The darkness creeps across the lake,
I used to be afraid of it,
Until Father told me that, if
You can't see them, they can't see you.

An owl hoots.

> Better drowned than duffers,
> If not duffers won't drown,
> No Father and no Mother around.
>
> Just me to see that we're okay,
> Just me.

An owl swoops past and disappears into the darkness.

> I'll navigate the starlit seas,
> They look to me to lead the way,
> Prove to Mother and Father that they
> Can trust their eldest son.
>
> Better drowned than duffers,
> If not duffers won't drown,
> No Father and no Mother around,
> Just me to see that we're okay,
> Just me.
>
> Better drowned than duffers,
> If not duffers won't drown,
> No, Father, I won't let you down,
> No, Father, I won't let you down.

ROGER (*speaking*). John! Are you coming? John?

JOHN. Don't worry. I'm here! Goodnight.

SUSAN *and* TITTY. Goodnight.

ROGER. Goodnighty, night-night.

Scene Twelve

The following morning. At the camp, JOHN *is sitting by the fire, boiling water for breakfast.* ROGER *is asleep in his tent.* SUSAN *and* TITTY *are asleep in their tent.* SUSAN *wakes up and looks at her watch.*

SUSAN. Titty? Titty? Buck up. It's really late.

TITTY. Late? What time is it?

SUSAN. It's half-past seven.

TITTY (*sitting up*). Half-past seven! But the war's started!

They rush out of the tent.

JOHN. Hello, you two.

TITTY. Why didn't you wake us?

JOHN. There was no need. Look at it.

SUSAN *and* TITTY *look out across the lake, which is bathed in sunshine.*

SUSAN. Oh. There's no wind.

TITTY. It's dead calm.

JOHN. And the barometer's steady.

ROGER *comes rushing out of his tent.*

ROGER. War! War! Everyone get ready for war!

TITTY. Forget it, Roger. There isn't going to be a war.

SUSAN. Not yet anyway.

ROGER. What? What do you mean?

JOHN. There's no wind, Roger.

SUSAN. We can't row all the way past Rio. And they can't row
    here.

ROGER. But I whistled for a wind!

TITTY. So did I.

SUSAN. Well, it didn't work this time.

ROGER. But that's not fair!

TITTY. It's a disaster.

JOHN. It could all change later in the day.

SUSAN. The wind might come. It's possible.

TITTY. But what will we do while we're waiting?

SUSAN. We could teach Roger to swim.

JOHN. We could clean *Swallow* and polish all her brass so she's
    fit for battle.

ROGER. I don't want to do that.

TITTY. Neither do I. Those are completely boring things to
    do.

SUSAN. Boring? I'm not having that. All we've wanted for
    weeks is to get here and do exactly those kinds of things.

ROGER. Well, now we don't want to. Now we want war.

SUSAN. And sometimes you can't have exactly what you
    want when you want it. (*Rallying them.*) Come on. We
    could collect firewood. I know – we'll go and see the
    charcoal burners. There must be lots of wood in their
    forest.

TITTY. You really think collecting firewood makes up for not
    going to war?

SUSAN. That's a terrible face, Titty. You'll stick like that if the
    wind changes.

TITTY. There isn't any wind.

Song – 'Let's Make the Best of It'

SUSAN.
> When plans go up in smoke,
> Don't sit around and mope,
> Find somewhere else to go,
> A new game to play.

TITTY (*speaking*). No.

SUSAN (*singing*).
> Come on, now, let's not build
> A mountain out of a molehill,
> We've got some time to kill,
> Why waste the day,
> Wishing it away?

TITTY (*speaking*). Why am I living?

SUSAN (*singing*).
> Let's make the best of it,
> Enjoy the rest of it,
> Let's make the best of it.

TITTY (*speaking*). I wish I was dead.

SUSAN *and* JOHN (*singing*).
> Don't make a meal of it,
> A great big deal of it,
> Just make the best of it,
> Let's make the best of it.

TITTY (*speaking*). I'd prefer to eat sand.

SUSAN (*singing*).
> How about hide-and-seek?

TITTY (*speaking*). No.

SUSAN (*singing*).
> I'll count to ninety-three.

TITTY (*speaking*). No, you won't.

SUSAN (*singing*).
>   The last one found can be
>   Queen of the island.

TITTY (*speaking*). I can't hear you.

ROGER (*singing*).
>   No, let's pretend we're in
>   The lair of the Cannibal King,
>   In his big pot stewing.

SUSAN *and* JOHN (*singing*).
>   Oh, Roger, why can't
>   You be less violent?

SUSAN (*speaking*). Come on then – what are we waiting for?

ROGER. Where are we going?

SUSAN. To see the charcoal burners.

TITTY. Boring. Boring. Boring.

They climb into Swallow *and sail off.*

SUSAN *and* JOHN (*singing*).
>   Let's make the best of it,
>   Enjoy the rest of it,
>   Let's make the best of it,
>   Don't make a meal of it,
>   A great big deal of it,
>   Just make the best of it,
>   Let's make the best of it.

They arrive at the CHARCOAL BURNERS' *camp, and approach cautiously. There are two* CHARCOAL BURNERS – *old men, hunched over a large fire. Behind them is a large wigwam-like tent.*

JOHN (*speaking*). Good morning. Is it all right if we watch?

CHARCOAL BURNER 1. We don't object.

JOHN (*looking at the fire*). What do you burn the wood for?

CHARCOAL BURNER 2. To make charcoal.

JOHN. To sell?

CHARCOAL BURNER 2. Aye. Folks use charcoal to make iron. It burns hotter than anything, see.

SUSAN. Why do you block the fire up like that?

CHARCOAL BURNER 2. The slower the fire, the better the charcoal.

CHARCOAL BURNER 1. He darts out like a snake – see – if you let him.

ROGER. And bites you.

CHARCOAL BURNER 1. Aye. If you're not careful.

SUSAN. Why doesn't it go out?

CHARCOAL BURNER 2. Once he's got a good hold you can cover him up, and the better you cover him the hotter he burns.

SUSAN. Could we do it with a little fire? Would it keep alight all night?

CHARCOAL BURNER 2. Aye. Cover him with damp clods of earth. He'll be alight in the morning, and he'll boil your kettle for you when you take the clods off.

SUSAN. I'll try that tonight.

They stare at the fire in silence.

TITTY. Don't you ever get bored?

CHARCOAL BURNER 1. Bored? What's bored?

SUSAN (*singing*).
> It's boring to be bored,
> What are we waiting for?
> I am declaring war,
> On scowling faces,
> Less than a week ago,
> We were all stuck at home,
> Now we're here on our own,
> In one of nature's
> Loveliest places.

SUSAN, JOHN *and* ROGER.
>Let's make the best of it,
>Enjoy the rest of it,
>Let's make the best of it,
>Don't make a meal of it,
>A great big deal of it,
>Just make the best of it,
>Let's make the best of,
>Enjoy the rest of,
>Let's make the best of it.

CHARCOAL BURNER 1 (*speaking*). Camping on the island, are you?

JOHN. Yes. How did you know?

CHARCOAL BURNER 1. When you see those girls...

CHARCOAL BURNER 2. The Blackett girls...

ROGER (*whispering*). The Amazons.

CHARCOAL BURNER 1. Tell them to give their uncle a warning.

TITTY. A warning?

CHARCOAL BURNER 1. Tell him to take care of his houseboat. Keep a padlock on the door.

JOHN. But why?

CHARCOAL BURNER 2. We hear things and see things.

CHARCOAL BURNER 1. Be sure he gets the warning today.

JOHN. We will.

TITTY (*to* JOHN). But we might not see the Amazons today.

JOHN. Then I'll take the message myself. I'll have to.

TITTY. How thrilling!

Scene Thirteen

Back on the beach on the island. JOHN *sets off in a rowing boat.*

ROGER. Good luck, Captain!

TITTY *and* SUSAN. Good luck! Good luck, John!

JOHN *is rowing towards* CAPTAIN FLINT*'s boat.*

Song – 'Navy Stroke'

JOHN.
>Navy stroke, navy stroke,
>Not too fast, not too slow,
>The proper way to row a boat,
>Navy stroke, navy stroke.

The other SWALLOWS *arrive back in camp. There is a forked stick stuck in the ground, with a note attached to it.*

SUSAN (*speaking*). Someone's been here.

TITTY. What?

JOHN (*singing*).
>Just give him the message,
>Turn and row away.

TITTY (*speaking*). It can't be the Amazons. They couldn't have rowed here.

JOHN (*singing*).
>Hope that I can find
>The proper words to say.

SUSAN (*speaking*). Oh, no. This is awful. It's from Captain Flint.

ALL. Captain Flint?

TITTY. Of all the nerve! To come into our camp when we're not here!

ROGER. What does it say?

SUSAN. 'Called to tell you that you had jolly well better leave my houseboat alone. If any of you dare to come near my houseboat again there'll be trouble. No joking.' And it's signed – 'James Turner'.

ROGER. So it isn't from Captain Flint. He's a naughty man, that James Turner.

SUSAN. He is Captain Flint.

TITTY. It's his secret name.

ROGER. What a beast!

TITTY. Oh, no! We have to stop John. Captain Flint will be so angry. (*Calling.*) John! John!

ALL. John! Ahoy there! Turn about! John!

JOHN (*singing*).
    Navy stroke, navy stroke.

TITTY (*speaking*). It's no use.

SUSAN. He's too far away to hear.

JOHN (*singing*).
    Pull your weight, set him straight,
    The grown-up way to row a boat,
    Navy stroke, navy stroke.

TITTY (*speaking*). Poor John. Oh, poor John.

JOHN (*singing*).
    Try to hold your nerve,
    And look him in the eye,
    Talk so you'll be heard,
    And always be polite.

    JOHN *has reached the houseboat.* CAPTAIN FLINT *is standing on deck. He has a suitcase next to him and is dressed in travelling clothes.*

CAPTAIN FLINT (*speaking*). Look here, did you find that note
I left for you? Did you read it? I take it you can read. Well, I
meant what I said. I told you to stay away from my boat, so
what do you think you're playing at, coming here again?

JOHN (*singing*).
   Just give him the message,
   Turn and row away.

CAPTAIN FLINT (*speaking*). Funny, was it, letting off that
firework on my roof? Come to take a look at the damage,
have you? Don't you dare try that again.

JOHN (*singing*).
   Hope that I can find
   The proper words to say.

CAPTAIN FLINT (*speaking*). Just be quiet. Lay to your oars
and clear out fast.

JOHN. It wasn't us.

CAPTAIN FLINT. Don't try to lie your way out of it. Who was
it, then? One of the younger ones? You're the biggest, you're
still to blame. Now, I have to go away tonight, but if anyone
comes messing with my boat while I'm gone, I'll know who
to blame. Believe you me. And there'll be hell to pay.

JOHN. It wasn't any of us!

CAPTAIN FLINT. Lies! Away with you! Go on! I don't want to
hear your denials. I don't like talking to liars!

JOHN. But I'm not a...

CAPTAIN FLINT. You're a liar! Now get out of here! Go on!

   JOHN *has turned bright red and struggles to contain his
   emotions. He rows back to the island.*

JOHN (*singing*).
   Navy stroke, navy stroke,
   Not too fast, not too slow,
   The proper way to row a boat,
   Navy stroke, navy stroke.

Scene Fourteen

JOHN *arrives back on the island. The others flock around him.*

TITTY. What happened? John?

SUSAN. What did he say when you gave him the message?

ROGER. Did you get to go on-board?

JOHN. I didn't give him the message. He wouldn't let me.

TITTY. Did you declare war?

JOHN. He called me a liar. He called me a liar.

> JOHN *walks away. It is clear that he wants to be alone.*

TITTY. What an absolute rotter Captain Flint is. I hate him.

SUSAN. Don't say that. Mother wouldn't like it.

TITTY. We shouldn't just attack his boat, we should sink his boat right now!

ROGER. Listen!

> *The music has brought the wind.*

Do you hear it? And look –

> *He points to the trees which are beginning to sway.*

SUSAN. The wind.

TITTY. The wind! It's the wind!

ROGER. John! John! It's the wind!

> JOHN *comes hurrying towards them.*

JOHN. I hear it! This is perfect timing. I reckon there's about two hours before dark.

SUSAN. What kind of wind is it?

JOHN. A southerly. That's a fair wind for us.

ROGER. Hurrah!

JOHN. There's no time to lose, crew. Gather round.

TITTY. What's the plan, Captain?

JOHN. The Amazons will see that it's a fair wind, but they'll think we won't launch an attack this late in the day.

SUSAN. Perhaps we shouldn't…

TITTY. They'll be on shore, feasting and sleeping off their drunken orgies.

JOHN. Three of us will sail to the islands off Rio and wait there until just before dusk. We'll need supplies.

SUSAN. Aye, aye.

JOHN. Then – if there's no sign of the enemy craft, we'll sail up the Amazon River to the boathouse. We'll cut out the Amazon and put a prize crew aboard her – that's you, Mister Mate – then we'll sail both boats back as fast as we can. Able Seaman Titty, how would you feel about staying here and lighting the leading lights for us?

TITTY. Staying here? On my own?

SUSAN. You don't have to, Titty…

TITTY. But I want to! I really want to.

JOHN. Good. That's settled then.

ROGER. What about me? What do I do?

JOHN. You can come along and be lookout.

SUSAN. Are you sure he shouldn't stay here? It will get awfully chilly on the lake when the sun goes down.

ROGER. I'm coming. If you try to leave me behind, I'll swim after you.

SUSAN. What – with one foot on the bottom?

JOHN. I'm sure he'll be fine.

SUSAN. Well, he'll have to wrap up well. Three of everything.

JOHN. Come on, then, everyone. We're going to war!

They put supplies and blankets on board Swallow.

Right. Everyone ready?

ROGER *comes out of his tent wearing three of everything.
He looks like a football, with his arms sticking out stiffly at
his sides.*

ROGER. Is this all right?

SUSAN. He ought to be warm enough like that.

JOHN. Last check. I've got my compass. That's essential.

SUSAN. You've got the matches, Titty?

TITTY. Yes. Have you got your torches?

SUSAN. Yes.

ROGER. Oh dear.

SUSAN. What?

ROGER. Mine's in my pocket.

SUSAN. Which pocket?

ROGER. The one at the bottom.

JOHN. Never mind. Here's the telescope, Titty. Keep a good
lookout. When you hear the signal…

TITTY. The hoot of an owl.

JOHN. Light the leading lights immediately.

TITTY. I will.

SUSAN. Are you sure you'll be all right on your own?

TITTY. Of course. I'll be Robinson Crusoe. I'll wear a blanket
for a goatskin.

JOHN. And don't fall asleep, whatever you do. If the lights
aren't lit, it'll be a disaster.

TITTY. I won't. I promise. I won't let you down.

JOHN. So, crew – to the ship!

They clamber aboard Swallow. TITTY *helps to push her off. They sail away.*

TITTY. Good luck! Swallows for ever! Hurrah!

SWALLOWS. Hurrah! Hurrah!

Scene Fifteen

TITTY. I've been marooned. 'Marooned.' What a wonderful word. 'She found herself marooned.' I must keep a log.

Song – 'Like Robinson Crusoe'

Since I could read I've longed to be like Robinson Crusoe.

(*Writing*.) 'The history and adventures of Titty Walker, castaway.'

She thinks for a moment.

The eighteenth of August, in the year of our Lord nineteen twenty-nine. This is my first day of being marooned upon this desert island and I am greatly content to be alone.

(*Singing*.) Making my home all on my own like Robinson Crusoe,
A castaway washed up one day upon a strange and faraway Deserted island.

No Susan to take care of you in *Robinson Crusoe*,
And Roger, he does not need me in *Robinson Crusoe*,
When there are five and you're the third,
You have to shout just to be heard,
I'm tired of shouting.

One sandy beach to softly tread on,
One grassy bank to rest my head on,
One little cloud to keep my eyes on,
One tiny ship on the horizon.

Don't rescue me, I want to be like Robinson Crusoe,
At least not yet, I've yet to get like Robinson Crusoe,
When I've a beard and gone quite mad,
Then you can come and take me back,
Back home to Mother,
My lovely mother.

Scene Sixteen

Swallow, *with* JOHN, SUSAN *and* ROGER *aboard, is on the lake, sailing towards the Amazon River. The sun is sinking low in the sky. Clouds are gathering and the wind is getting up. There is a clap of thunder in the distance.*

SUSAN. Captain John? Did you hear that? I think the wind might be bringing a storm.

JOHN. Look! There's the mouth of the Amazon River.

SUSAN. I hate to say it, but I think we should turn back.

JOHN. No. We're not going back until we've captured the *Amazon*.

ROGER. Of course we're not going back!

SUSAN. But we can't sail in a storm. And it'll start getting dark soon. It's too dangerous. Mother wouldn't like it.

JOHN. Stop fussing, Susan. What does it matter if we get a bit wet? This is a war, not a picnic.

SUSAN. I'm not going to sail *Amazon* in the dark, and not in a storm. I've never even sat in her.

ROGER. I'll sail her. I love storms!

JOHN. See? Even Roger's not afraid.

SUSAN. Don't be silly – you know he doesn't understand.

ROGER. I do understand. I do speak your language, you know.

JOHN. Prepare to lower the sail.

SUSAN. No. We should go back and try again in the mor–

JOHN. This is mutinous talk, Mister Mate.

SUSAN (*shocked*). No, it's not. It's just...

JOHN. Is that was this is? A mutiny?

ROGER. I'm not mutinying.

JOHN. If you ruin this now, it'll go down as the greatest mutiny
in history.

ROGER. We should make her walk the plank.

JOHN. It'll be recorded in the ship's log and you will face shame
and infamy. And what is more, your name will forever be
linked with cowardice. Is that what you want, Mister Mate?

Pause.

SUSAN. No. No, it's not.

JOHN. Very well. Lower the mainsail.

SUSAN. Aye, aye, Captain.

ROGER. Aye, aye, Cap'n!

JOHN. Quietly. From the moment we row into that river, we're
in enemy territory. We have to be completely silent and
completely alert.

ROGER. Can I row?

JOHN *and* SUSAN. No.

JOHN. Mister Mate will row – as quietly as ever she can. I shall
steer. You go forward, Ship's Boy, and be lookout. Remember,
we're looking for a large boathouse on the right bank.

ROGER. With a skull-and-cross-bones over the door.

There is a distant rumble of thunder.

Thunder!

JOHN *glances at* SUSAN, *who says nothing.*

JOHN. Let's make this raid swift and efficient. Sweeps in the water, Mister Mate. Right hand down.

SUSAN. Aye, aye.

JOHN. No – wait a moment.

JOHN *scoops water into his hand and wets the row locks.*

ROGER. What are you doing?

SUSAN. He's wetting the row locks so they don't squeak.

JOHN. Right. Let's go.

They row Swallow *into the Amazon River. Everything changes – no more squally wind and open space – they are now in a sheltered narrow channel, with tall reeds on either side. There is the occasional rumble of thunder, and it's almost completely dark.*

Unseen by the SWALLOWS, *the* AMAZONS, *hidden in the reeds, watch the* Swallow *row past. They snigger.*

SUSAN (*suddenly*). What's that? I thought I heard laughter.

ROGER. So did I.

JOHN. I didn't hear anything. Concentrate, crew.

They continue up the river. There is a sudden loud flap of wings in the reeds.

ROGER. Aah!

JOHN *and* SUSAN. Shh!

They hear a quack as a duck flurries by.

SUSAN. Just a duck.

ROGER. I thought it was the harpy.

JOHN. Eyes ahead, Ship's Boy.

They continue.

This is very good. We've got them, I'm sure of it. They'd have challenged us long before this if they'd seen us.

ROGER (*whispering*). There it is! I see it! There!

JOHN. That's it.

SUSAN. The boathouse.

JOHN. Quiet now. Easy all.

SUSAN stops rowing. They drift towards the boathouse.

ROGER (*loudly*). The skull-and-cross-bones!

JOHN *and* SUSAN. Shh!

JOHN. That's it all right.

ROGER. It's a huge skull. I've never met anyone with a head as big as that. He wouldn't be able to hold it up.

JOHN. Can you see in? Can you see *Amazon*?

ROGER. There's a big boat in there.

SUSAN. That must belong to their parents... I mean, the barbarians. Will our mast clear the beam?

JOHN. Yes. Just. That's it. Gently now.

They row into the boathouse.

Can you see the *Amazon*?

SUSAN. Don't bump the launch, Captain.

ROGER. She isn't here.

JOHN. What?

SUSAN. She must be.

JOHN takes out his torch and turns it on. He scans the boathouse. There is an empty space on the far side where Amazon *should be.*

JOHN. I don't believe it.

There is a large envelope pinned to the wall. ROGER *spots it.*

ROGER. What's that?

He grabs it.

SUSAN. Give it to me.

ROGER *hands it over.* SUSAN *and* JOHN *examine it.*

ROGER. What does it say?

JOHN. 'To the Swallows.'

JOHN *opens it and takes out a note.*

ROGER. What does it say?

JOHN. It says… It says… 'Ha, ha'.

SUSAN. 'Ha, ha.' Signed, 'The Amazon Pirates. Nancy Blackett, Captain. Peggy Blackett, Mate.'

ROGER. 'Ha, ha.' So, it's a sort of joke?

SUSAN. They must have suspected we would come and they've moved the *Amazon*.

JOHN. Of all the low-down, mean, villainous tricks!

There is suddenly a huge flash of lightning overhead.

ROGER. Wah!

SUSAN. Oh, no! What do we do now?

Scene Seventeen

On the island. It is now completely dark. There is a huge clap of thunder very close by.

TITTY. Oh my goodness! Ah! – A tree just fell down on Cormorant Island! Keep calm. Only a silly old storm. It'll soon pass over. Come on, Titty. Titty Walker, castaway. I'm not afraid of storms.

Suddenly she hears the long call of an owl. 'Tu-whooooo. Tu-whooooo.'

Oh! Oh! That's the signal! I'm coming! I'm coming!

Frantically she feels for her torch and finds it. She switches it on, and uses it to light her way to the harbour.

There, she uses matches to light the leading lights.

Keep your hand steady… There. Now, come on. Come on, *Swallow*.

Suddenly a big owl flies over her head, calling: 'Tu-whooooo! Tu-whooooo!'

It sweeps away into the darkness.

A real owl… Perhaps it wasn't them after all.

But then she hears the sound of a boat on the lake, and the distant sound of chanting.

AMAZONS (*chanting, off*). Amazons, Amazons, Amazons, Amazons, Amazons…

TITTY. But… what's that?

The Amazon *is approaching the harbour.*

NANCY. Leading lights! Now that is a cunning idea.

PEGGY. Nice of them to think of us, I say.

NANCY. Couldn't have been more helpful. Line her up, Peggy. And row her in!

TITTY. Oh no. Oh, what have I done?

AMAZONS (*singing*).
> We'll cut out your gizzards with a blunt pair of scissors for starters,
> Use your skull as a cup and your lily-livered guts for garters,
> We'll lop off your ears so while you can hear, heed this warning,
> Better marshall your defences, our battle commences in the morning!
> This means war!

There is a terrific thunderclap, as the storm hits.

End of Act One.

ACT TWO

Scene One

Aboard the Swallow, JOHN, SUSAN *and* ROGER, *are making their way back up the river to the lake. It is pitch dark. There is a flash of lightning.*

ROGER. One, two, three, four...

Thunder.

Four! It's almost overhead!

SUSAN. Oh, this is awful!

JOHN. Stop complaining, Mister Mate. It can't be far to the lake now. Can't you row faster?

SUSAN. My oars keep getting stuck. There are so many water lilies.

JOHN (*muttering to himself*). What a fool those Amazons have made of me. What a fool.

Keep a sharp lookout for any sign of a mast, Ship's Boy, they might have hidden Amazon in the reeds.

ROGER. Keep a lookout? I can't even see my hand!

Lightning. ROGER*'s hand (which he is holding in front of his face) is suddenly illuminated, along with everything else.*

One, two, three...

Thunder.

Three!

SUSAN. Oh, I knew we shouldn't have come!

ROGER. The wind. That's the wind!

JOHN. We're out! We've reached the open sea. Torches out, Mister Mate, let's see what we can see.

ROGER (*singing*). A sailor went to sea sea sea...

Lightning. One, two – thunder.

SUSAN (*speaking*). Oh, John. It's so dark. There's nothing. We can't see anything.

ROGER. I can see lights over there.

JOHN. Rio lights. That'll be helpful.

SUSAN. Helpful for what? What are we going to do?

JOHN. Head back to the island.

SUSAN. But do you think we can find it?

JOHN. Hoist the mainsail!

SUSAN. In the dark?

JOHN. Come on!

SUSAN and ROGER do so, with some difficulty.

I'll put her to the starboard tack and keep her very full. We want to be sure that we're clear of the rocks off the promontory.

Lightning. Thunder.

ROGER. Oooh. I don't know if I like that. What would happen if we got hit by the thunder?

SUSAN. We won't be. We'll be all right, Roger, I promise.

Suddenly, the rain begins to pour down. The wind gets stronger. The storm is right overhead.

Oh no!

JOHN. Take cover, you two!

SUSAN goes to ROGER.

ROGER. I'm getting very wet.

SUSAN (*grabbing a blanket*). Come under here. Quickly!

ROGER. Wouldn't Titty have liked this?

SUSAN. What?

ROGER. Sailing about in a real storm with no idea where we're going.

SUSAN. Don't be silly. We do know where we're going.

She leaves him and goes to JOHN. *The storm is on top of them now.*

John? What can I do?

JOHN. Hold the torch over the compass.

SUSAN does so.

It's no good. We're keeling over – it won't work. I think that's east but I can't be certain.

SUSAN. Should we try to get into Rio?

JOHN. I'm not sure. I'm not sure what we should do. I just have to try… to keep her afloat.

Swallow *battles the wind, and* JOHN *and* SUSAN *struggle to keep control of her.*

(*Suddenly.*) Do you hear that? Trees! Wind in the trees – we must be close to the shore!

SUSAN. We're being blown!

JOHN. What's that? Rocks? Down with the sail! Grab the yard as it comes!

SUSAN does all this as fast as she can.

Quick! Quick!

SUSAN. There's something close here! It's here! Pull! Pull your left! It's… Oh!

There is a thump as Swallow *hits something.*

JOHN. Rocks!

ROGER. What was that?

SUSAN. No – it's a landing stage. We've hit a landing stage!

JOHN. Grab hold of it! Quick! Grab it!

SUSAN. I've got it!

JOHN. Wait! Hold on! I'll tie her up!

> JOHN, *holding the painter, feels his way onto the landing stage. The rain begins to ease off as the storm passes.*

ROGER. Are we all right?

SUSAN. John? John?

JOHN. It's all right. We're secure. There's a sign here.

SUSAN. What does it say?

JOHN. 'Private. No landing.'

SUSAN. Oh.

JOHN. Never mind. It's an emergency. We'll ignore it. This must be one of the little islands off Rio.

SUSAN. The storm's passing. Thank goodness.

JOHN. But we can't go back on the lake. I can't navigate in this darkness. We'll have to stay here until first light.

SUSAN. But what about Titty?

JOHN (*sheepish*). She'll be fine. She has a tent. And food.

> SUSAN *goes to* ROGER.

SUSAN. Are you all right, Roger?

ROGER. That was fun, wasn't it?

SUSAN. Yes. Are you cold?

ROGER. I'm as cold as a polar bear who's lost his furry coat.

SUSAN. Here, have this blanket.

She gives him a dry blanket.

Do you want some chocolate?

ROGER. Yes please! How much can I have?

SUSAN. Quite a lot. In fact, have all of it.

ROGER. Thanks! This just gets better and better!

SUSAN *goes back to* JOHN.

SUSAN. One of the blankets is soaked.

JOHN. I'll go without. You go and settle down now.

SUSAN. Poor Titty. I wish we hadn't left her. I can't believe we left her.

SUSAN *starts to go back to* ROGER.

JOHN. Susan – I'm sorry.

SUSAN. It's all right…

JOHN. No. It's not all right. I've been beastly. And I think I just came very close to being the biggest duffer there ever was. I'm really, really sorry.

SUSAN. Apology accepted. Perhaps we'd better not tell Mother about this.

JOHN. I won't if you won't. At the very first sign of light, we'll go back to the island. Lie down with Roger now. Get some sleep.

SUSAN. What about you?

JOHN. I'm going to stand guard. And watch for the light.

Scene Two

The harbour. Wildcat Island. The storm has just passed overhead. TITTY *emerges from her hiding place in the bushes.*

TITTY (*whispering*). Eighteenth of August in the year of our Lord nineteen hundred and twenty-nine. A most terrible and calamitous event has overtaken me: viz; a crew of dastardly pirates has landed upon my island and has spread about to search. And I fear, alas, that they be cannibal pirates too, who will eat me all up in a most foul and hideous feasting. I feel I have been most foolish and neglectful of my island, and I fear there will be, soon, great wrath and insults poured down upon my sorry head from those who relieth upon me: viz; John, Susan and Roger.

Thunder as the storm retreats.

The storm abateth. What shall I do? What shall I do? I have no hatchet, nor any musket to set about them with. Nor can I dig a pit to trap them in for I want for any spade or digging... thing. What shall I do? What shall I do? But wait... wait, says I...

There is another thunderclap. Then NANCY*'s voice can be heard approaching.*

NANCY. Not here. Told you. Back to the harbour.

TITTY. They return. This is it. It must be now. It must be now.

TITTY *runs to the* Amazon. *She unfastens the painter and climbs inside. She picks up the oars.*

Use the leading lights. One above the other. One above the other.

Slowly, she rows Amazon *out of the harbour, safely negotiating the rocks. It is pitch dark, but she keeps going –*

rowing straight out towards the middle of the lake. One of the leading lights goes out.

There goes one of the leading lights. It must be the lantern I carried from the camp. Thank providence I left when I did.

The AMAZONS' *voices are suddenly heard from the distant island.*

NANCY. Hey! Where's our ship?

PEGGY. Hey! Where's *Amazon*? Hey!

NANCY. Peggy, you donkey. You didn't tie her up properly and now she's drifted.

PEGGY I did tie her up.

NANCY. So where is she?

PEGGY. Someone's taken her. I told you I saw a light moving about.

NANCY. There's no one on this island except us. And now we're stuck here. All night!

PEGGY. Well, whose fault is that, Cap'n Nancy?

NANCY. And now we've lost the war, you swab.

PEGGY. It was your plan, you poxy pig.

TITTY rows a little further then stops, exhausted. The thunder is distant now and the rain has stopped, but it is still windy and cold. TITTY turns on her torch and feels in the boat for an anchor. She finds it.

TITTY. Check it's fast. John always says to check it's fast.

She checks. It is. She looks back to the island.

They could never reach me here. I must be almost at Cormorant Island by now.

She lowers the anchor over the bows, until Amazon *is brought up with a little jerk. She notices some chocolate and eats some. She takes out her log.*

The eighteenth of August in the year of our Lord nineteen
hundred and twenty-nine. I find myself now quite secure
upon this pirate vessel which I have captured for my prize.
So I shall settle me down and payeth no heed to the very
black darkness which surrounds me, nor the strangeness of
the water beneath me. Nor shall I think at all about my
mother. And I shall resteth me.

TITTY *falls asleep.*

Song – 'Titty's Dream'

CHORUS.

>Stealers steal and creepers creep,
>Over oceans dark and deep,
>Through the revolving doors of sleep,
>Stealers steal and creepers creep.

>Talkers talk and takers take,
>Dreamers are dreaming that they are awake,
>Keep hearing voices on the lake,
>Talkers talk, takers take.

>Steal away and go to sleep,
>It's very late to be sailing,
>Even explorers ought to be
>In their beds, sound asleep.

TITTY *dreams. In her dream, she sees her* MOTHER,
*dressed as Queen Isabella, sailing by on a royal barge. She
sees* JOHN *in the uniform of a naval captain, saluting and
waving goodbye. She sees the* AMAZONS *dancing round a
huge cooking pot, hooting like owls and stamping their feet,
and she sees* ROGER'*s head come peeping out of the pot.
She sees* MR JACKSON *running about dressed as Man
Friday.*

She sees two PIRATES *rowing by in a boat. They have stripy
T-shirts and eye patches and bandannas.*

PIRATES.

>Stealers steal and creepers creep,
>Going to bury the treasure we've taken,

> While the world is sound asleep,
> Got to be finished before the dawn's breaking,
> Best to stay out of the way,
> Hiding in shadows and quietly quaking,
> Even though it's plain as day,
> We're fanciful, fictional, all in your mind.

PIRATE 2 (*speaking*). No one comes to this island except those crazy birds. It'll be safe here.

PIRATE 1. That's land. Get out and pull her in. Now give me a hand with this box.

PIRATES (*singing*).
> Talkers talk and takers take,
> You won't remember us when you awaken.

TITTY.
> Um, excuse me, I'm awake!

PIRATES.
> You think you're awake but you're very mistaken,
> It's a dream.

TITTY.
> It seems so real.

PIRATES.
> A simple mistake anyone could be making,
> Can't you see we're fantasy,
> We're fanciful, fictional, all in your mind.

PIRATE 2 (*speaking*). You can tell by the weight it's something worth having.

PIRATE 1. Nobody will find it now. We'll come back when the fuss has died down.

TITTY (*singing*).
> But tell me, if you don't exist,
> How come we're having this weird conversation?

PIRATES.
> Listen, missy, it's like this, we
> Only exist in your imagination.

TITTY.

> Yes, I guess that would explain
> Why you are singing and dancing and making
> All the strangest transformations,
> Fanciful, fictional, all in my mind…

(Speaking, in her sleep.) Nobody will find it now…

No… Poor Roger. Poor Roger.

She sleeps on.

Scene Three

Daybreak. TITTY, *curled up in the* Amazon, *gradually becomes aware of voices, as* Swallow *approaches.*

JOHN. It's definitely Amazon. She's not drifting. She's at anchor.

SUSAN. How strange. I don't believe there's anybody in her.

> TITTY *suddenly raises her head over the gunwale.*

Titty!

JOHN. Titty! But… Are you on your own?

TITTY. Yes. I captured her. I captured *Amazon*!

JOHN. Hurrah!

SUSAN. Well done, Titty! Well done!

> ROGER*'s head appears from inside* Swallow *for a moment.*

ROGER. Titty? Where? Oh, yes. Hello, Titty.

He disappears again and goes back to sleep. JOHN *brings* Swallow *alongside* Amazon. SUSAN *grabs* Amazon's *gunwale.*

JOHN. However did you do it? Where are the Amazons?

TITTY. They've got our camp. They've got Wildcat Island. I'm really sorry. I couldn't help it. There was an owl and I thought it was you, and then I lit the lights and they...

JOHN. It doesn't matter, because we've got their ship.

SUSAN. So we win. We just have to get her into the harbour.

JOHN. Well done, Titty. What a first-rate sea dog you are!

TITTY. And I used the leading lights to row through the rocks. And I rowed out here and dropped anchor. And then I... I must have fallen asleep, and then I heard these...

JOHN. But *Amazon* is our prize. That's all that matters. (*Glancing at* SUSAN.) That, and that we're all safe.

SUSAN. Yes. Especially that.

JOHN. *Swallow* is flagship after all. Titty, I'm coming aboard.

JOHN climbs aboard Amazon.

Now then, Able Seaman, will you take the tiller to sail her across? She's your prize, you know.

TITTY (*amazed*). Really? Me? I mean, aye, aye, Cap'n!

She takes the tiller.

JOHN. Are you ready, Mister Mate?

SUSAN. Ready, Captain.

JOHN. Then let's sail our fleet into port.

They sail towards the island.

Song – 'Conquering Heroes, Victory Chorus'

SWALLOWS.
> We are conquering heroes,
> We are famous explorers,
> We are mighty conquistadors,
> And what's more we've won the war.

They are close to the island and can see the AMAZONS *more clearly.*

SUSAN (*speaking*). Look! Look!

JOHN. What are they doing?

SUSAN. It's one of our blankets. They're waving it.

TITTY. It's a white flag. They're surrendering.

ROGER. It's not very white.

TITTY. It's meant to be.

JOHN. We'll soon find out.

TITTY. Cap'n Nancy looks like she's doing another war dance.

ROGER. Perhaps she needs the toilet. I do.

SUSAN. Be quiet, Roger.

SWALLOWS (*singing*).
>
> We're the kings of the castle,
> We have done the impossible,
> We have captured the *Amazon*,
> And now that's done we've won the war.

The AMAZONS *are at the lookout point, jumping up and down.*

JOHN (*shouting across*). Do you surrender?

NANCY. We do. We do. We jolly well do. But buck up.

PEGGY. Buck up, won't you?

JOHN. No trickery?

NANCY. Honest pirate.

JOHN. Honest Injun too?

PEGGY. Honest anything you like, just bring her in.

JOHN. We'll take her into port. We only win when she's in our harbour.

NANCY. Put your back into it, Mister Mate. Wave it harder.

PEGGY. How come it's me who has to wave the white flag?

NANCY. Captains don't wave white flags.

PEGGY. Yes they do. It's captains who do the surrendering. It was your silly plan that lost the war.

NANCY. Silence, swab, or I'll hang you from the yardarm.

PEGGY. You wave it. Take the shame, Captain Nancy.

The fleet heads for the harbour.

SWALLOWS (*singing*).
 We are conquering heroes,
 We have two, you have zero,
 It will go down in history,
 A famous naval victory for the *Swallow*,
 Swallow!

Scene Four

TITTY *sails* Amazon *into the harbour.* SUSAN *brings* Swallow *in behind her. The* AMAZONS *clap, and help to pull the boats in.*

JOHN. Captain Nancy, which ship is flagship?

NANCY. *Swallow* is. And earned it. But do buck up. We're supposed to be in bed. We have to get home before we're called for breakfast or we'll really catch it.

SUSAN. Oh, I see. Sorry.

JOHN. You'll never do it.

PEGGY. Yes we will. The wind's fair and it's getting stronger.

NANCY. The sun's only just rising and Dad and Mum are lazyboneses in the holidays.

The SWALLOWS *disembark.* TITTY *is last.* NANCY *shakes her by the hand.*

By thunder, Able Seaman, I wish you were in my crew. When I realised what you'd done all on your own, I could have swallowed the anchor.

TITTY. Anyone would have done the same.

NANCY. Not in that storm. Peggy wouldn't.

PEGGY. Yes, I would, if I had to.

NANCY. You would not. She was scared to death of that thunder.

PEGGY. I still would have done it.

NANCY. Jelly-guts.

PEGGY. Blabbermouth.

NANCY. Milksop.

PEGGY. At least I knew there was someone on the island. I said there was but she said…

NANCY. Silence your scurvy tongue or I'll hang you from the yardarm!

SUSAN. Have you got time for some tea?

NANCY. Wish we had, but we'd better get under way.

    NANCY *and* PEGGY *board* Amazon.

JOHN. But what was your plan?

NANCY. I'll tell you later. It was a good one.

SUSAN. I hope you don't get into terrible trouble.

NANCY. We won't. We're old hands. We jump into bed with all our clothes on and pull the covers up high.

PEGGY. And I pretend to snore.

TITTY. I'll get the painter!

    TITTY *unfastens the painter.*

ROGER. But you will come back, won't you?

NANCY. Try stopping us. Now that we've settled who's
flagship, we're ready to attack Captain Flint. We're yours to
command, Commodore John.

JOHN. Fleet assembles at eleven hundred hours. We attack the
houseboat today!

TITTY. Hurrah!

ROGER. And make him walk the plank!

PEGGY. We've stockpiled ammunition. Wait till you see what
we've got.

NANCY. Firecrackers and arrows! Lots of them!

JOHN. Ammunition! Why didn't I think of that?

SUSAN. We'll collect feathers for your arrows.

TITTY. And pine cones for cannonballs.

ROGER. And I'll make spears!

PEGGY. We'll be back as soon as we're in the clear.

JOHN. I'll work out a plan of campaign.

NANCY. He'll curse the day he was born!

TITTY. Swallows and Amazons for ever!

ALL. And death to Captain Flint!

The AMAZONS *have worked their way out of the harbour,
and they sing 'The Amazon Pirates' as they sail away.*

SUSAN. Good luck!

NANCY*'s voice can just be heard.*

NANCY. Watch it, Peggy, you donkey. Keep her steady.

Scene Five

In the camp, SUSAN *is tidying up the breakfast things.* TITTY *is counting pine cones into a pan.* JOHN *is at the lookout point, scanning the lake through the telescope.*

TITTY. Twenty-one, bang! Twenty-two, boom!…

ROGER *arrives with a stick twice as big as himself. He charges up to* SUSAN, *letting out a war cry.*

ROGER. Ahhh…!

SUSAN. Don't be silly, Roger.

ROGER. This is my invincible spear!

SUSAN. Just put it back where you found it.

TITTY. Twenty-six. That should blow him to smithereens!

JOHN. Ship ahoy!

ROGER. They're here! They're here!

TITTY. At last!

ROGER *runs to* JOHN.

ROGER. I see them!

JOHN. But… No. It's not them. It's not *Amazon*.

ROGER. But it's coming here.

JOHN. Yes, but it's a rowing boat. It looks like a barbarian.

ROGER. Barbarian! Barbarian!

JOHN. In fact… it really looks like… a policeman.

ROGER *charges to the camp.*

ROGER. Policeman! Policeman!

SUSAN. A policeman?

TITTY. Coming to our island?

SUSAN. Quick – clear up this mess. Titty, tidy your hair. Roger, stand up straight and try to look like you haven't done anything.

ROGER. I haven't done anything.

JOHN *joins them.*

JOHN. He's landed.

SUSAN. Oh, John, you don't think…

JOHN. Mother? But she couldn't have found out so soon.

SUSAN. And she wouldn't have sent a policeman, would she?

The POLICEMAN *walks into the camp. He is sweating after the long row, and looks very annoyed.*

Good morning, Officer. Would you like some tea?

POLICEMAN. No, I would not, miss. I'm here on a very serious matter. Too serious for tea.

JOHN. What is it?

SUSAN. Did our mother send you? Because we know we…

POLICEMAN. I shall ask the questions, thank you very much.

ROGER. You're welcome.

POLICEMAN. Now then. (*Taking out a notebook.*) Are there any more of you?

JOHN. No. It's just us four.

POLICEMAN (*writing*). 'Us four…'

TITTY. Actually there are lots more of us, spread all over the island and…

SUSAN. Be quiet, Titty.

POLICEMAN. And what are you doing here, I should like to know?

JOHN. We're camping. This is our camp.

POLICEMAN. Names?

JOHN. I'm John Walker. This is Susan, Titty and Roger.

POLICEMAN. Address?

TITTY. Here. We live here.

SUSAN. We're staying at Jackson's Farm with the Jacksons. Our mother is there.

ROGER. And Fat Vicky. She's the baby.

POLICEMAN (*writing*). 'Fat… Vicky…'

JOHN. Mother knows we're here.

POLICEMAN. And where were you last night?

Pause. JOHN *and* SUSAN *look at each other.*

JOHN. We were on the lake. At least…

SUSAN. It was the storm, you see. We couldn't get back so we had no choice, we had to…

POLICEMAN. You were out on the lake?

TITTY. Yes. But I was in a different boat.

ROGER. She was in *Amazon*.

POLICEMAN. So you admit that you were out on the lake all night?

JOHN. Yes. But…

POLICEMAN. And you had no adults with you?

SUSAN. No. But…

JOHN. I say, what's this about, Officer?

POLICEMAN. A crime was committed on the lake last night.

SUSAN. A crime?

POLICEMAN. And you have been named as chief suspects.

TITTY. What?

POLICEMAN. A crime involving trespass… a crime involving vandalism… a crime involving theft.

JOHN. Theft?

All the SWALLOWS *speak at once.*

But we've never taken anything that didn't belong to us.

SUSAN. We wouldn't dream of stealing.

ROGER. We're not thieves.

TITTY. We've never stolen anything in our lives.

POLICEMAN (*shouting above them*). Quiet!

They fall silent.

Thank you very much.

ROGER. You're welcome.

JOHN. Officer…

POLICEMAN. I shall have to go and speak to your mother, and then I shall want you to answer some more questions. Down at the station.

The SWALLOWS *are shocked.*

TITTY. You can't do this.

POLICEMAN. Oh, I can do whatever I like, young miss. Especially when I've been woken up at five in the morning and had to go rowing up and down this lake and chasing after youngsters who ought to be kept indoors. I want you off this island and back at Jackson's Farm. Understood?

JOHN. Yes.

The POLICEMAN *goes to his boat. He takes out a large white sign and a mallet. He walks back into their camp and fixes the sign into the ground. The sign reads 'No Children'.*

He goes back to his boat and gets in.

POLICEMAN. And that applies to all the islands on this lake.

He rows away. The SWALLOWS *stand in silence.* ROGER*'s lip starts to tremble.*

SUSAN. Don't cry, Roger.

ROGER. Will we have to go to prison?

TITTY. No, we will not! It's all a lot of nonsense. We haven't done anything wrong.

SUSAN. Unless... John, you don't think we could have damaged that landing stage when we bumped into it?

JOHN. I don't... I don't think so. We would have noticed this morning, wouldn't we?

SUSAN. We did rather crash into it. But theft... Think, everyone: has anyone taken anything at all that didn't belong to them?

JOHN *and* TITTY. No.

ROGER. I don't think I have. I'm very sorry if I have.

TITTY. Of course he hasn't.

JOHN. It's all right, Roger.

TITTY. You know, when I was on the lake last night, I did have the strangest dream...

SUSAN. Oh, don't start with your dreams now, Titty.

TITTY. But in this dream, at least I think it was a dream, there were two pirates...

SUSAN. For goodness' sake, Titty. We don't want to listen to any of your ridiculous stories. We're in trouble. Proper, serious trouble.

TITTY. But...

SUSAN. Just be quiet!

Pause.

What shall we do, John?

JOHN. I think we had better start packing up the camp.

ROGER. No! I don't want to go!

JOHN. We don't have any choice. It's over. Let's pack up and then go and face Mother.

Sadly, they begin to pack.

Song – 'Swallow's Packing Up'

SWALLOWS.
> A big tin box of books and writing paper – a small aneroid barometer,
> And other things that need to be kept dry – like nightclothes,
> I won it as a prize at school – three biscuit tins with bread and tea and sugar,
> No more bread, just a couple of eggs – separately wrapped for fear of smashes,
> A frying pan, a saucepan and a kettle – mugs and plates and spoons and forks and knives,
> Two groundsheets with tents wrapped up inside – half a seed cake,
> A long coil of stout grass rope – two sacks stuffed with blankets and rugs,
> A tin of corned beef, tins of sardines – I think we've got all that we need.

Suddenly they hear the AMAZONS *approaching from the direction of the harbour. Reprise of* AMAZONS *chanting.*

NANCY (*speaking*). Ahoy there! We bring blood-curdling news.

PEGGY. Thunderous news!

NANCY. Timber-shivering news… But what's happening?

SUSAN. We have to leave.

ROGER. Something terrible's happened.

NANCY. What are you talking about?

PEGGY. Has someone got the plague? Or yellow fever?

TITTY. Worse than that.

JOHN. We've been accused of theft.

NANCY. Theft?

ROGER. A policeman came. We've got to go to the police station.

SUSAN. He's gone to talk to our mother.

TITTY. And look…

PEGGY. 'No Children'? But…

TITTY. It's the end of everything.

SUSAN. Apparently there was a crime committed on the lake last night and…

PEGGY. We know. That's what we were going to tell you.

NANCY. It's Captain Flint's houseboat. It was broken in to!

JOHN. The houseboat!

NANCY. He was away but he got called home first thing this morning.

PEGGY. The motorman passed by and saw the cabin door banging about and a terrific mess on deck.

NANCY. And something precious has been taken.

JOHN. Captain Flint! So, that's who's accusing us!

TITTY. We should have guessed.

ROGER. I hate Captain Flint! I hate him!

JOHN. We had nothing to do with it. I swear.

NANCY. Gaskets and bowlines – we know that!

SUSAN. John, if it was the houseboat that was broken in to…?

JOHN. The message! Of course!

NANCY. What message?

SUSAN. We went to see the charcoal burners…

JOHN. And they asked us to give a message to you to give to Captain Flint.

SUSAN. They said they had heard some rumours, and that someone might try to break into his houseboat.

NANCY. Thunder and lightning!

JOHN. I couldn't deliver the message because… well, I just couldn't.

SUSAN. And we haven't had the chance to tell you until now.

JOHN. If only I'd managed to give him the message. If only.

NANCY. Well, that's jolly decent of you – I should say it serves him right that his boat's been burgled, seeing as how he's accused you of being thieves.

ROGER. And we might have to go to prison.

SUSAN. We won't, Roger.

PEGGY. First he becomes a misery-guts and ignores us all summer, then he turns into the nastiest, scurviest barbarian there ever was!

NANCY. But why does Captain Flint think it's you? That's what I don't understand. What, in the name of Davy Jones, has made him think that you'd go near his boat?

TITTY. It's because…

JOHN. Don't, Titty.

SUSAN. No, tell them, John. I think you should.

NANCY. Tell us what?

PEGGY. Tell us what?

JOHN. It was the firework – at least, that's how it started.

SUSAN. He thought it was us who set off the firework on his boat.

JOHN. He saw us sailing past not long afterwards.

SUSAN. He was very angry.

ROGER. He shook his fist like this… (*Demonstrates.*) Horrible.

PEGGY. Oh, no!

SUSAN. He came here while we were out and left a note.

ROGER. A nasty note.

JOHN. And then when I rowed out to his boat to give him the message, he… well, he just wouldn't listen.

TITTY. It was worse than that. He shouted at John and called him a liar.

PEGGY. What?!

They all look at NANCY. *She has gone very red and livid, and is breathing very hard.*

NANCY. Right. Right. Peggy?

PEGGY. Yes, Cap'n!

NANCY. You know what this means.

PEGGY. Yes, Cap'n! And I'm right behind you.

NANCY. Commodore John, I need pencil and paper. Immediately.

ROGER. I'll go!

He runs off and gets some.

NANCY. And a piece of your charcoal, Mister Mate.

SUSAN. Charcoal? Aye, aye!

She goes to the fire and fetches a piece. ROGER *returns and hands the paper and pencil to* NANCY. NANCY *sits and begins to write.*

TITTY (*to* PEGGY). What is she doing?

Song – 'The Black Spot'

PEGGY.

> The black spot is what you get,
> When a pirate is upset,
> A decision you'll live to regret,
> Though not for too long.
>
> The black spot awaits all those,
> Double-crossing slimy toads,
> Who have contravened the pirate code
> (Done their crew wrong).

NANCY *puts the mark of the black spot onto the letter. Everyone gasps.*

> Let the black spot be attached,
> To an arrow and dispatched,
> Through the porthole of the entry hatch,
> Of his galleon.

NANCY.

> Wish me luck and wave goodbye,
> No, First Mate, just me this time,
> Sometimes sorrows come in single spies,
> Not battalions.

She heads off to the harbour. They all follow.

PEGGY.

> When the black spot he is shown,
> He will gasp and he will groan,
> He will scre-ee-ee-ee-eam and go
> All to pieces.
>
> And there's much, much worse in store,
> For the uncle who ignored,
> His two swee-ee-ee-ee-eet adorable nieces
> (You and me, sis…)

NANCY *rows off in* Amazon.

They run to the lookout point.

When you're by the black spot cursed,
Your blood boils and your veins burst,
You will drink and drink and drink,
And still your thirst is unquenchable.

You get pustules on your face,
On your legs, arms, chest and waist,
You will itch and itch and itch,
In places unmentionable.

You're afflicted with the pox,
Bits of you keep falling off,
And you get a very nasty cough,
Which is never nice.

You get nosebleeds that won't stop,
All your extremities rot,
Anybody who receives the spot
Pays a heavy price.

The SWALLOWS *join in and get more and more carried away. Only* JOHN *remembers that they're supposed to be watching* NANCY. *He looks out towards the houseboat, and his eyes grow wide.*

JOHN (*speaking*). Look, everyone… Everyone!

Everyone stops, except SUSAN.

PEGGY. She's done it! She's coming back!

JOHN. Susan!

SUSAN *stops singing.*

PEGGY. But so is he.

ALL. What?

TITTY. He's coming after her. Captain Flint is coming after her.

JOHN *takes up the telescope.*

ROGER. He's not really coming, is he, Susan? Is it a joke?

JOHN. He is coming. He's in a boat and he's rowing like a steam engine.

ROGER. Oh, no! Oh, no! I don't want him to come.

SUSAN. It's all right, Roger. Calm down.

TITTY. There's nothing he can do to us.

PEGGY. Except toast us and eat us alive.

ROGER. Oh, no.

SUSAN. Don't say things like that, please.

PEGGY. Go to it, Nancy! Come on!

ALL. Go to it! Go on, Nancy!

PEGGY. Keep it up, Nancy!

TITTY. Swallows and Amazons for ever!

ALL. And death to Captain Flint!

They run to the landing place, as NANCY *arrives, very much out of breath.*

NANCY. We're in for it now, lads!

ROGER. Don't let him land! Don't let him land!

CAPTAIN FLINT *arrives and tries to ground his boat beside* Amazon, *but the* AMAZONS *push it off again. He tries again, but they won't let him land.* ROGER *hides behind* SUSAN.

NANCY. Off with you! Go on!

PEGGY. We don't want you here!

TITTY. Go away! You're not allowed on our island!

SUSAN. Titty…

PEGGY. You've had the black spot.

TITTY. You're an enemy!

FLINT (*singing*).
    Parley, parley, maybe we can talk this through…

NANCY (*speaking*). The parley rule doesn't work when you've had the black spot.

PEGGY. You're a pox-ridden outcast and you're doomed for ever.

JOHN. We don't like talking to bullies.

CAPTAIN FLINT *appeals to* JOHN.

Song – 'The Parley – Flint's Apology'

CAPTAIN FLINT.
> Young man, please listen to me,
> I've got something I must say,
> I've treated you so poorly,
> Please don't treat me the same way,
> Do you think that you could forgive,
> A very foolish man?
> I questioned your integrity,
> Ignored all that you said to me,
> I'm sorry, and I beg to be forgiven,
> Please, shake hands?

JOHN (*speaking*). Parley then. My name is John Walker, Master of the ship *Swallow*. Who are you?

CAPTAIN FLINT. My name is James… But, I say, why, in your black spot, did you call me 'Captain Flint'?

PEGGY. Because Titty said you were a retired pirate.

CAPTAIN FLINT. Why, so I am.

NANCY. This is Able Seaman Titty.

CAPTAIN FLINT. So it was you who knew the dark secret of my pirate past? How clever of you.

TITTY. I saw your parrot.

CAPTAIN FLINT. Ah. I am Captain Flint.

NANCY. And this is the Mate of the *Swallow* and her name is Susan.

CAPTAIN FLINT. How do you do, Mister Mate?

NANCY. And this is Roger, their Ship's Boy.

ROGER. How do you do?

CAPTAIN FLINT. I've been a ship's boy myself. It's a hard life.

ROGER. You can say that again.

PEGGY. What was stolen from the boat, Uncle Jim? I mean, Captain Flint?

CAPTAIN FLINT. My book. That's what. My book which I've been slaving over all summer. And missing out on all the fun for. And, do you know, if they'd taken anything else, I wouldn't have minded at all.

NANCY. Well, now it's gone, so you can make up for lost time. I say we have a war.

ROGER. Yes!

SUSAN. But we can't.

PEGGY. Why not?

CAPTAIN FLINT. I'm afraid the Mate's right. I'm afraid even a skirmish is out of the question until we've got ourselves out of this fix. Now, you say in this shockingly terrifying note here, that the charcoal burners tried to warn me.

JOHN. Yes. They had heard some talk in the village.

ROGER. Barbarian talk.

CAPTAIN FLINT. I see. Then the first thing I must do is find that policeman and tell him to go and speak to them. And then I must take him with me to see your mother and tell her how very wrong I've been about you.

SUSAN. Thank you. That would be such a help.

JOHN. It would be a start.

ROGER. And then will the policeman take his sign down?

CAPTAIN FLINT. I hope so, Ship's Boy, but I can't be sure. He can be quiet a curmudgeonly old so-and-so when he wants to be.

NANCY. Like you.

CAPTAIN FLINT. Yes. I really am most awfully sorry.

CAPTAIN FLINT *holds out his hand to* JOHN, *who shakes it*.

JOHN. Apology accepted.

TITTY. You're a dirty turncoat, Captain John.

SUSAN. Titty!

ALL (*singing*).
Parley, parley, surely we can talk this through,
Parley, parley, talk with me, I'll talk with you.

CAPTAIN FLINT (*speaking*). So, are we all friends now?

NANCY. Friends! We don't want to be friends!

CAPTAIN FLINT. I see. Enemies then.

NANCY. Mortal enemies.

CAPTAIN FLINT. Good idea.

TITTY. What would happen if someone found your book? I mean, if someone thought they knew where it might be?

NANCY. That would make that barnacle-sucking policman take his sign down and we could have a hideous war immediately!

CAPTAIN FLINT. Wait, Captain Nancy. Why do you ask that, Able Seaman?

TITTY. Because, you see, when I had to sleep in the lake on *Amazon*… I was having these strange dreams, and then I saw these pirates rowing by and…

SUSAN. Oh, Titty, don't. Please, don't take any notice, Captain Flint. She often makes up stories and…

TITTY. But I'm not making it up. It might have been a dream, but the two pirates had stolen some treasure and they were saying how heavy it was and how they would have to hide it and then…

PEGGY. But Uncle Jim's book wouldn't be heavy.

NANCY. Heavy-going, maybe.

CAPTAIN FLINT. But it was! By jiminy, it was! It was with my typewriter and all my old diaries and locked up in my big cabin trunk! I'd put a huge padlock on – that's why the thieves took it, you see – they thought there must be something valuable inside.

TITTY. That's it then! They took it to Cormorant Island and hid it there!

SUSAN. Oh, please don't listen to her.

CAPTAIN FLINT. But I think we should listen to her. Which is Cormorant Island, Able Seaman?

TITTY. The small one between here and your boat.

ROGER. Where the harpies live.

FLINT. They left it there, you say?

TITTY. Yes. They said 'until the fuss has died down'.

CAPTAIN FLINT. Come on then, crews – to the longboats! No time to lose.

SUSAN. But...

JOHN. She does have a very vivid imagination.

CAPTAIN FLINT. Sign of great intelligence, I say. If you're mistaken, Able Seaman, fear not. But it has to be worth a try.

TITTY. Yes. Thank you.

CAPTAIN FLINT. To Cormorant Island!

NANCY. Cormorant Island it is!

CAPTAIN FLINT *and the* AMAZONS *rush off.* SUSAN *and* JOHN *give* TITTY *reproachful looks.*

SUSAN (*reprimanding*). Titty.

Then they leave.

TITTY. Come on, Roger.

ROGER. Couldn't you have said another island?

TITTY. No. You do believe me, don't you?

ROGER. Yes. But I'm not happy. Not happy at all.

She leads him off.

Scene Six

The two boats, with everyone aboard, sail up to Cormorant Island.

TITTY. Look, Roger – the harpies are flying away. We've scared them off.

ROGER. Good.

FLINT. Do you think this is where the Pirates landed, Able Seaman?

TITTY. Well… there were a lot of rocks where they landed. They crashed against them.

JOHN. The whole island is full of rocks, Titty.

FLINT. Let's spread out.

NANCY. Be on your guard, everyone! There could be land crabs or alligators or enemies of all kinds!

PEGGY. The treasure may be buried beneath hundreds of dead men's bones!

TITTY. Or the pirates might have set traps and snares! We may all lose our lives finding it!

SUSAN. Do be quiet, Titty. You're making it worse.

CAPTAIN FLINT. Anything, anyone?

PEGGY. A load of smelly old fish bones.

ROGER. Victims of the harpy!

JOHN. I don't think there's anything here.

NANCY. Wait a minute – what's this?

They rush to where she's standing by the water. She holds up a scarf – rather wet and muddy.

TITTY. It's one of theirs! The pirates were wearing those! This must be where they came ashore. I must have been moored just over there.

JOHN. You were, come to think of it.

CAPTAIN FLINT. Excellent. An excellent clue.

TITTY. So they pulled the chest this way, across this shingle and then… and then…

PEGGY. Did they dig a hole?

TITTY. I didn't hear much digging.

SUSAN. So where is it, then?

PEGGY. Look! Tracks!

They rush to her.

JOHN. They are!

PEGGY. Something was dragged this way.

NANCY. Something heavy.

ROGER. Follow them!

They do so.

PEGGY. This is where they stop.

TITTY. Nothing. I don't understand.

SUSAN. Wait a minute, what's this?

She picks up a torn piece of paper.

ALL. What does it say? What does it say?

SUSAN. 'Aca… pul…' Half of it's missing…

NANCY. 'Acapul'… It doesn't mean anything.

JOHN. Acapul… co! Acapulco!

CAPTAIN FLINT. Acapulco! It's one of the labels from my
    trunk! Now we're really onto something!

PEGGY. It must be buried.

ROGER. Perhaps they put a big X over the spot! All look for an
    X!

NANCY. But if Titty didn't hear much digging…

CAPTAIN FLINT. Nowhere obvious to hide it.

JOHN. Unless… What happens when a big tree falls down?

TITTY. It leaves a big hole! The tree! The tree!

*They all rush to the dead tree. Behind it, its roots sprawl up
into the air, leaving a big hole at the base.*

JOHN. Lift all the stones away!

They do so. Suddenly the trunk can be seen.

TITTY. It's here!

ROGER. We've found it!

CAPTAIN FLINT. That's it all right! My cabin trunk! I say!

SUSAN. I don't believe it.

NANCY. Hurrah!

ALL. Hurrah! Hurrah!

PEGGY. All help get it out.

*They pull it out of the hole. It is a large trunk covered in
labels from all* CAPTAIN FLINT*'s travels around the world.*

ROGER. It's got a huge padlock.

CAPTAIN FLINT *takes a key from his pocket and opens it.
He lifts out his precious manuscript.*

CAPTAIN FLINT. Good as new.

JOHN. So you weren't dreaming, Titty. I'm sorry.

SUSAN. So am I. Really sorry. I should have believed you.

TITTY. Apologies accepted.

ROGER. Not very interesting treasure.

CAPTAIN FLINT. Oh, there's treasure and treasure. Able
    Seaman, all of you, I can never thank you enough. And this
    changes everything. The crime is solved. And you, who were
    once the suspects, are the heroes of the hour.

ROGER. Will the policeman take the sign down?

FLINT. Oh, yes, Ship's Boy, I'm sure he will.

PEGGY. And can we attack your boat now?

FLINT. Attack my boat? I tell you what, tomorrow will see the
    greatest sea-battle of all time. The Battle of Houseboat Bay!

ALL. Hurrah!

NANCY. You do mean a real battle? You will defend yourself to
    the death?

FLINT. I most certainly shall. I shall be ready to repel boarders
    and sink both your ships. The scuppers will be red with
    blood.

ROGER. Crikey.

FLINT. Shall we say, three o'clock?

JOHN. Three o'clock it is.

PEGGY. I hope you've got a good plank.

FLINT. Now, can I borrow the *Amazon*, Captain Nancy, to get
    this back to my ship?

SUSAN. But what are you going to do about the real thieves?

NANCY. They should be hanged on Execution Dock!

ROGER. Hanged and drawn and quartered!

FLINT. Do you know… I'm not going to do anything at all. I only wanted my book back, and now, thanks to you, I have it. If the policeman tracks down the culprits, I'm sure he'll have a quiet word with them.

JOHN. They'll be disappointed enough when they come back and find the treasure gone.

TITTY. Let's leave them a note!

FLINT. Good idea.

JOHN. Yes. Who has paper and pen?

ALL. Not me. No.

JOHN. Then we'll carve it – on this.

> JOHN *picks up a flat piece of driftwood, and takes out his penknife.*

NANCY. It' ll have to be short, then.

SUSAN. What about 'Ha, ha'? That's bound to annoy them.

> PEGGY *and* NANCY *smirk.*

FLINT. Very good, Mister Mate. I think that's it.

> JOHN *starts to carve it out.*

ROGER. And… and then we could put… we could put… 'You are very nasty, bad pirates…'

> *Unseen by* ROGER*, a cormorant is coming up behind him.*

SUSAN. Roger…

ROGER. And we, the Swallows and Amazons, are the terror of these seas, and…

TITTY. Roger…

ROGER. And when we find out who you are we will come to you in the black of night and…

> *The cormorant nudges him with his beak.*

And…

He turns. The cormorant screeches.

Ah!

ROGER *runs. The cormorant chases him. The others laugh.*

Help! Get away from me! Get away from me!

SUSAN. Roger, calm down.

ROGER. Help!

He runs into the sea. The cormorant comes after him.
ROGER *starts to swim. The cormorant loses interest.*

JOHN. Roger? You're swimming!

ROGER. I am? I am!

He is so excited, he forgets to swim for a second, and starts
to sink, but then immediately rights himself.

Hurrah!

ALL. Hurrah! Well done, Roger!

Scene Seven

The following afternoon. The Battle of Houseboat Bay.

CAPTAIN FLINT *is standing on the deck of his houseboat. He*
is wearing a sun helmet, and has a red handkerchief tied around
his middle. His parrot is on his shoulder.

The houseboat is flying a green flag with a picture of a large
walrus on it.

CAPTAIN FLINT *scans the surrounding waters.*

CAPTAIN FLINT. Come on – show yourselves! I know you're
    out there! Come on, you pestilent sea dogs, come and do
    your worst! If you had the pluck of a weevil in a biscuit
    you'd show yourselves!

Suddenly, the Swallow *and the* Amazon, *with their crews aboard, emerge from the haze, singing. They advance on the houseboat.*

Aha! That's more like it! Prepare to swim with the fishes! Them that die'll be the lucky ones!

The boats draw near. ROGER *suddenly blows a loud whistle repeatedly, and the attack begins.*

ALL. Hurrah! War! Attack!

They begin to hurl their arrows at the houseboat.

FLINT. Ha! I have an answer for that!

He immediately fires his cannon at them.

Take that, you swabs!

TITTY. And you take that, you old codfish!

TITTY *and* SUSAN *begin to hurl pine cones at* CAPTAIN FLINT. *Most of them fall short, but a few reach him, and he pretends to be caught in their explosions.*

FLINT. Ah! Ah!

ROGER *throws twigs.*

ROGER. And that! And that!

JOHN. Slacken away your mainsheet, Amazon! Come alongside!

NANCY. Aye, aye.

CAPTAIN FLINT. I'm still standing! I've got you now!

ROGER. He's going for the cannon again!

PEGGY *throws firecrackers.*

PEGGY. See how you like these!

CAPTAIN FLINT. Ah! Ah! Dastardly! Devilish!

JOHN. Prepare to board!

NANCY. Aye, aye!

The boats are now alongside.

CAPTAIN FLINT. Marauders, Polly! Prepare to repel! Prepare
to repel!

POLLY. Pretty Polly!

JOHN. Cutlasses at the ready! Attack!

The SWALLOWS *and* AMAZONS *pour onto the houseboat.*
CAPTAIN FLINT *grabs two cushions and begins to whirl
them round his head –*

CAPTAIN FLINT. Ah… h!

They charge at him, and he bashes them over the head.
PEGGY *spots his stockpile of cushions.*

PEGGY. Here! Here!

She throws them out and they all attack back.

NANCY. At him, all hands!

TITTY. Take that and that and that!

CAPTAIN FLINT *is disarmed.*

CAPTAIN FLINT. Ah! Ah! Ah!

JOHN. Get his legs!

CAPTAIN FLINT. Ah! Oomph!

He is brought crashing to the deck.

ALL. Hurrah! Got him!

CAPTAIN FLINT. Help, Polly, help! Reinforcements required!
Peck their eyes out! Feed them to the piranhas!

TITTY. Here, Polly, you come to me…

She holds out her arm. Polly comes willingly and squawks.

POLLY. Pretty Polly!

The others cheer.

CAPTAIN FLINT. Treacherous bird!

NANCY. Yield!

CAPTAIN FLINT. Never!

NANCY. Yield!

CAPTAIN FLINT. Not while my flag still flies! Walruses!
Walruses for ever!

PEGGY and ROGER run off and take down the green flag.

SUSAN. Your flag is struck – we've won!

CAPTAIN FLINT sits up and sees that the flag is gone.

CAPTAIN FLINT. Why, so it is.

He lies down again.

JOHN. Surrender!

CAPTAIN FLINT. I surrender. I surrender.

NANCY. Bind the prisoner!

PEGGY. Bind him! Bind him!

They set about binding his arms behind his back.

*At this moment, a rowing boat appears. MOTHER and Fat
Vicky are aboard, and MR JACKSON is rowing.*

SUSAN. It's Mother!

TITTY. You mean, Queen Isabella! Oh, look!

*MOTHER is wearing a flowing veil and coronet of flowers.
MR JACKSON has been forced to wear a tea cosy on his
head, by way of an Elizabethan hat.*

They all look.

NANCY. Thunder and lightning!

CAPTAIN FLINT. I say!

MOTHER and MR JACKSON board the houseboat.

JOHN. Your Majesty, your arrival is most timely.

MOTHER. What news of battle, my brave conquistadors?

SUSAN. We have captured the most evil and notorious pirate, Captain Flint.

MOTHER. Bring him before me!

They pull CAPTAIN FLINT *to his feet and shove him to the rail so that he is facing* MOTHER.

CAPTAIN FLINT. Good day, Your Worshipful Majesty.

NANCY. Silence, dog!

TITTY. Bow! Make him bow!

He does so.

MOTHER. What are his crimes?

NANCY. The worst is treachery – all summer he has been in league with the barbarians.

PEGGY. Desertion! He deserted us.

TITTY. Invasion! He came into our camp when we weren't there.

ROGER. Fist-shaking! He did – (*Shakes his fist.*) this to us.

FLINT. Did I really? I'm most awfully so–

PEGGY. Silence, swab!

SUSAN. Slander! He called John a liar.

JOHN. Yes, but we've made peace over that.

TITTY. It doesn't matter. His crimes are manifold.

CAPTAIN FLINT. Jolly good word.

TITTY. Thank you. Your Majesty, shall the prisoner be made to walk the plank?

CAPTAIN FLINT. Walk the plank! Oh, I say...

ALL. Yes! Yes! The plank! Make him walk the plank!

POLLY. Pretty Polly!

CAPTAIN FLINT. Treacherous bird!

JOHN. Your verdict, Your Majesty – yea or nay?

CAPTAIN FLINT. If I could just plead for…

PEGGY. Silence!

MOTHER. What do you say, everyone? Yea or nay?

ALL. Yea! Yea!

MOTHER. Then I say… Yea!

ALL. Hurrah! Hurrah! To the plank! To the plank!

They drag him to the plank.

MOTHER. But it is Princess Vicky's will that the prisoner's hands be untied, that he might swim for it.

ROGER *and* TITTY (*disappointed*). Oh!

SUSAN. That's right. Do what Princess Vicky says.

ROGER. Princess Fat Vicky.

They untie his hands.

CAPTAIN FLINT. Thank you, Your Majesty. Most grateful, Your Majesty.

NANCY. Now walk!

CAPTAIN FLINT. Oh, dear. Can't we…?

PEGGY. Walk!

He edges back a little way along the plank. After a moment his weight makes it tip a little.

CAPTAIN FLINT. Aah!

They all laugh.

NANCY. Walk, you son of a sea-calf!

He edges back until he is at the end.

CAPTAIN FLINT. Mercy! Mercy!

MOTHER. No mercy!

CAPTAIN FLINT. But, I say, you aren't really going to make me do it, are you?

ALL. Yes! Walk!

CAPTAIN FLINT. But there are sharks in there – hundreds of them.

ROGER. Good!

ALL. Walk! Walk! Walk!

He steps back and tumbles into the water. There is an enormous splash. They all laugh. Then they rush to the side.

ROGER. Where is he?

SUSAN. He can swim, can't he?

TITTY. Bubbles!

He comes up, spluttering and blowing water. More laughter.

CAPTAIN FLINT. Sharks… nibbling… oh, no!

He goes under again. Then he comes up, shouting.

Rope! Rope! Please! A rope!

SUSAN *throws him one.* CAPTAIN FLINT *struggles to get out of the water.*

JOHN. We present you with this captured vessel as your prize, Your Majesty.

MOTHER. I thank you most heartily, Captain John.

NANCY. Commodore John. He's Commodore for the battle.

MOTHER. And I thank you too, great *Amazon* pirates, whose daring deeds I have heard spoken of.

CAPTAIN FLINT *approaches, dripping wet, and makes a low bow to her.*

CAPTAIN FLINT. At your service, Your Majesty.

MOTHER. So, you have survived, Captain Flint.

CAPTAIN FLINT. To fight another day.

SUSAN. Would you like a towel?

CAPTAIN FLINT. Oh, thank you.

She hands him one. ROGER *throws his arms around* MOTHER.

ROGER. Welcome aboard, Your Majesty!

MOTHER. Why, thank you, Ship's Boy.

TITTY. We missed you.

MOTHER. I missed you too.

TITTY *takes the 'pearl' from her pocket and gives it to* MOTHER.

TITTY. This is for you. It's a precious pearl. It looked better when it was wet.

MOTHER. It's beautiful. Thank you.

ROGER (*suddenly*). I swam! I swam!

MOTHER. Did you? Without your foot on the bottom?

ROGER. Yes! Didn't I?

ALL. He did. We saw him.

JOHN. He swam faster than we ever thought he would.

MOTHER. Then in that case…

She brings out a penknife from her pocket.

PEGGY. Ooh. That's a nice one! Pearly handled. Better than ours, Nancy.

MOTHER. Please kneel, Ship's Boy.

He does so. MOTHER *'knights' him.*

I dub you Sir Roger of Jackson's Farm…

ROGER. No, Cormorant Island. Because that's where I did it.

MOTHER. I dub you Sir Roger of Cormorant Island. Arise, Sir Roger.

He does so. Everyone claps and cheers.

ROGER. I'm a knight! Now you all have to do what I say!

SUSAN. Don't be silly, Roger.

CAPTAIN FLINT. And I have a little ceremony of my own to perform – if that's all right, Your Majesty?

MOTHER. By all means.

CAPTAIN FLINT. Well, it's more of a bestowal really. Able Seaman Titty, you were so brave in helping me to recover my treasure that I should like you to have a treasure of your own.

He holds out Polly to her.

Here – take Polly.

TITTY. You don't mean…?

CAPTAIN FLINT. Yes. With your permission, Your Majesty, I'd like Titty to keep him. He's really taken a shine to her and vice versa.

ROGER. Crikey.

TITTY. Oh, Mother, can I?

MOTHER. Is he house-trained?

CAPTAIN FLINT. Oh, absolutely.

MOTHER. Then permission is granted. That's very kind.

TITTY. Oh, thank you! Thank you, Captain Flint. But won't you be lonely without him?

CAPTAIN FLINT. A little, I daresay. But he's a young bird and should have a young mistress. And I'm away on my travels again soon, and he'd be much better off with you.

TITTY. I'll take such good care of him.

POLLY. Pieces of eight!

They laugh.

NANCY. That's the first time he's said that!

MOTHER. I declare the expedition of the *Swallow* a great triumph. All of you appear unscathed by your adventures and it seems I may tell your father, the King, that none of you are duffers after all.

JOHN *and* SUSAN *exchange a look.*

JOHN. No. None of us are.

MOTHER. But now the time has come for me to recall my brave explorers to the court.

TITTY. Oh, no!

MOTHER. Where a great feast is being prepared for you, and we all eagerly await the tales of your heroic adventures. Isn't that right, Signor Jackson?

MR JACKSON. Si.

JOHN. Three cheers for Queen Isabella!

ALL. Hurrah, hurrah, hurrah!

Scene Eight

Back on Wildcat Island. Early evening. The AMAZONS *have helped the* SWALLOWS *to pack up their camp, and it is now empty.* SUSAN *approaches from the landing beach.*

SUSAN. Everything's loaded and stored, Cap'n John.

JOHN. Good work, Mister Mate.

Pause.

That's it then.

TITTY. I've just noticed something.

ROGER. What?

TITTY. The sign's gone.

ALL. Oh, yes.

NANCY. It'll make good firewood.

PEGGY. You will come again next summer, won't you?

SWALLOWS. Yes. Yes, of course we will.

ROGER. Try stopping us!

NANCY. We've got so much to do. We've got to explore the high ranges.

PEGGY. And prospect for gold.

JOHN. And sail to the Azores.

ROGER. And catch monkeys.

SUSAN. And take a canoe down the Amazon.

TITTY. And cross the Baltic Sea.

NANCY. Let's make an oath that we'll come back next year and the next year and the next, and that everything will be the same.

PEGGY. Except that we'll have new adventures.

TITTY (*looking at the parrot*). And a new crew member.

NANCY. Yes.

She puts her hand in the middle of the group.

I swear.

They all follow suit – putting their hands on NANCY*'s.*

JOHN. I swear.

PEGGY. I swear.

TITTY. I swear.

ROGER. I swear.

SUSAN (*hesitating*). But Mother says that nothing can ever stay the… I swear.

Pause. JOHN *looks about.*

JOHN. Goodbye, Wildcat Island.

ROGER. Goodbye, Wildcat Island.

TITTY. Goodbye, camp. When we've gone, someone else may discover it.

NANCY. If anybody tries to take it, we'll barbecue them, don't worry about that.

PEGGY. We'll see off any invaders.

SUSAN. But you thought we were invaders once – and look how it all turned out.

They all smile.

JOHN. Cap'n Nancy?

NANCY. What orders, Cap'n John?

JOHN. The fleet sets sail, and steers north.

NANCY. Aye, aye. All aboard, shipmates!

The SWALLOWS *and* AMAZONS *climb aboard their boats and set sail. They sing* 'Swallow' *and 'The* Amazon *Pirates', which weave together and build until…*

The End.